Pascal's Provincial Letters

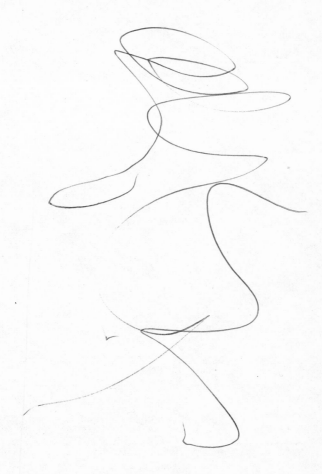

Pascal's Provincial Letters

An Introduction

Walter E. Rex

HOLMES & MEIER PUBLISHERS, INC.
IMPORT DIVISION
101 Fifth Avenue, New York, N. Y. 10003

ISBN 0 340 20203 3

First published 1977

Printed in Great Britain for Hodder and Stoughton Educational, a
division of Hodder and Stoughton Ltd, Mill Road, Dunton Green,
Sevenoaks, Kent by Elliott Bros. & Yeoman Ltd, Liverpool L24 9JL

Contents

Chapter I

The Historical Background of the 'Provincial Letters'

These witty and eloquent Letters by Blaise Pascal have been called the first masterpiece of French Classicism, and whether or not we accept this statement, we do know that few works of Pascal's time were so highly esteemed by the critics of the Classical age. Boileau thought them the only work by a modern author that was actually superior in kind to anything written in ancient Greece or Rome; and his opinion on the matter was related by Madame de Sévigné, herself an ardent enthusiast for the 'petites Lettres'. Charles Perrault, in his famous book comparing the Ancients and the Moderns, could not describe them without appealing to all the virtues most appreciated in his time: 'pureté . . . noblesse . . . solidité . . . finesse . . . agrément . . .' According to Voltaire, when Bishop Bossuet was asked if there were any work from another hand he himself would wish to have written, there was just one: '*Les Lettres Provinciales*.' Even Louis XIV was said to have laughed at one of them, despite his profound hostility towards the cause they represented.

Nor were the 'Provincial Letters' destined to dry out and ossify as seventeenth-century French period pieces. The pungency of their irony, the freshness of their comic characters, the almost impudent way they made one laugh at matters formerly thought so grave that even a smile was forbidden, the astonishing relevance of the questions they asked, the eloquence of their moral concern—all conspired to give these letters an import and a topicality that reached far beyond the particular circumstances in which they were born. They began turning up in causes that must have had their devoutly Christian, devotedly royalist author groaning in his tomb at St Etienne-du-Mont: during the aftermath of the Glorious Revolution, the English used them, in translation, to stir up hatred against France. They became a favourite work of the eighteenth-century anti-Christian *philosophes*, and in some respects both Montesquieu's *Lettres persanes* and Voltaire's *Lettres philosophiques* owe as much to Pascal as to any other single author. But Pascal would have been pleased at least that they were constantly reprinted in France during the first half of the eighteenth century as anti-Jesuit propaganda, since he had certainly intended them to be damaging to the Society of Jesus. And he would have taken special pride in their being cited as prime evidence by Abbé Chauvelin in his harangue to the Paris Parlement, for this was a critical moment in the great trial of the Jesuits that ended with their expulsion in 1762.[1]

Among the books we actually read for pleasure today, these Letters are the sole survivor of the religious controversies of seventeenth-century France, and to have thus endured represents no mean achievement. For, although the majority of works in any domain are inevitably forgotten by posterity simply through the process of natural selection, in religious controversies of this period in France the number of forgotten volumes swells into a mountain several times more massive than all the productions of belles lettres combined.[2] Nothing seems to have absorbed the age of Classicism so much as arguing about religion, and, viewing the variety of its productions, one wonders whether there was anything at all in Christianity that was not debatable: controversies on 'pure love' of God, on 'physical premotion' and free will, on attrition, on schism, on Papal infallibility, on the impious theological consequences of Cartesianism, on the authority of 'Tradi-

[1]See Dale Van Kley, *The Jansenists and the Expulsion of the Jesuits from France, 1757—1765* (New Haven and London, 1975) p. 123.
[2]See Henri Martin, *Livre, Pouvoirs et Société*, 2 vols. (Geneva: Droz, 1969), esp. Vol. II.

tion', on pagan virtue . . . and the list has barely begun. In the century of Corneille and Molière, theology, even more than belles lettres, remained for many the choice vehicle through which to discuss the great issues of life, and for some of the contemporaries of Louis XIV religious controversy—even more than politics, where the great issues were ruled out from the start—enabled them to give vent to the fiercest, and the noblest, of their passions: to their indignations, their hatreds, their loyalties, their grim determinations, their sublime resolves. Thanks almost entirely to Pascal's 'Provincial Letters', the most interesting of the controversies of this era, the great debate between the Jansenists and the Jesuits, remains alive for us today.

Early Jansenism

The word 'Jansenist' was never an officially accepted Catholic designation, as the word 'Jesuit' was. The title was informal and sometimes even derogatory, the way the word 'Calvinist' had been. It designated the doctrinal disciples of the Flemish theologian Cornelis Janssens, Bishop of Ypres, usually known by his Latin name, Jansenius. Jansenius was born in 1585, and he died in 1638, just two years before the publication of his great work, the *Augustinus* (1640), the main rallying point for the movement named for him, but which he himself never lived to see.

The *Augustinus* is a vindication of the doctrine of St. Augustine against what Jansenius thought to be the corruptions of recent theologians, particularly of Jesuits such as Molina and Lessius. The work is remarkable for many reasons, not the least of them being the astonishing mastery Jansenius displays as a tactician. First he slowly moves in upon the defences of his opponents and, with infinite patience and subtle argument, proceeds to demolish so completely their every inconsistency, their every false assumption, their every dubious thought, that the reader has nothing left to cling to, and finds himself helplessly listening to the dry, cold voice of the Bishop of Ypres as he lays bare, beyond all question or appeal, the austere verities of St Augustine on sin, predestination and grace.We will later have to take a closer look at some of these doctrines, but we may note here that such an icy intelligence could hardly be expected to generate much enthusiasm in our own era: we are too secular, and we have learned too much from Dr Freud. Yet to the generation of 1640, in the midst of the seventeenth-century Catholic religious reforms, this enormous volume seemed—to some at least—quite radiant with truth: it called upon them, amid the worldly corruption of their time, to make a deep inner commitment of themselves to a life of the spirit which was undefiled. Because this appeal was so lofty, and its manner of presentation so intelligent, Jansenism attracted (as most of their Jesuit contemporaries could not) some of the finest sensibilities of the age.

The centre of the movement in France was the Abbey of Port-Royal,[1] a convent for women situated in a valley some twelve miles southwest of Paris. Later there was a second Port-Royal established in Paris itself; but it was the first one, known as Port-Royal des Champs, that became famous—probably the most celebrated convent in modern literature. As of 1636, its principal spiritual director was the Abbé de Saint-Cyran, an early friend of Jansenius, a man deeply committed to the cause of Augustinianism. In 1638, for reasons both political and theological, Saint-Cyran was imprisoned by Richelieu, thus providing Jansenism with its first martyr. The best known Abbesse of Port-Royal was la mère Angélique Arnauld, of the great Arnauld family, the prime-movers of Jansenism after 1640. Her brother, Antoine Arnauld—often called '*le grand*' Arnauld—sometimes sojourned close by the Abbey, in what came to be a thriving community of pious persons, both laymen and clerics, who went there informally to study, meditate or write, and who were celebrated as 'les solitaires de Port-Royal'. Even apart from their theological productions, the achievements of these Jansenists are remarkable: they founded 'little schools' for children and, somewhat in the modern spirit, tried to imbue their pupils not merely with know-

[1]Cf. René Taveneau, *La Vie quotidienne des Jansénistes* (Paris: Hachette, 1973).

ledge but with a true love of learning: to make their Greek school book less awesome, they entitled it 'Le jardin des racines grecques'; in their Latin grammar they gave French translations of the Latin rules—not then the usual practice—and the work was an instant success both in France and abroad. Their 'Logic' was based mainly on Cartesian principles, a decided innovation for the time, and its presentation is so clear, and the examples so appealing, that it is still reprinted and read today. They produced a translation of the Bible, the famous 'version de Mons'; they engaged in countless religious controversies—unavoidably, since their reforms had aroused an army of opponents.

Jansenist Doctrines

Theologically, Jansenism drew much of its vigour from a deep and sometimes highly emotional awareness of man's continuing sinfulness, *le péché actuel*. Whenever they speak of this topic, as they constantly do, one finds—unrelieved by any of the picturesque flashes that occasionally brighten the pronouncements of Calvin, or, for that matter, the Anglican Book of Common Prayer—an accent of curious intensity, as if they were saying that here in fact was the touchstone of their belief, the matter they cared about most and that was most intimately connected with the life they lived. They use a number of traditional images to describe mankind in the throes of sin: sometimes they write of an infinite lassitude and weakness, an inability to rise up and be well; or of being bowed down to earth, or imprisoned in darkness; sometimes they speak of being broken, crippled or deformed, or even, occasionally, of diseases: of a contagion, a blight polluting all existence. Or again, one finds water imagery, suggesting the endless ebb and flow of human sinfulness. But the concept, perhaps because of its closeness to them, was not easily conveyed in pictures and analogies: the hideous reign of concupiscence, man's perverted love of things terrestrial that indeed blinded him to the good, making him a helpless prey to the tyranny of the senses and condemning him to sin, is difficult to depict as it functions, for it is above all an inner thing; the 'prison' is the heart itself that will not love God—the tides of concupiscence overwhelm man from within.

To the seventeenth-century Jansenists, the true 'proofs' of their theology—when they were called upon to justify themselves— lay not only in the Scripture, St Augustine, and the doctrines of the 'Primitive Church', but in what were for them the realities of psychological experience; and if they clung so tenaciously to one form of Augustinian Christianity it was because it seemed to them to subsume not only the possible glories, but above all the piercing agonies of the existence they knew. It is also true that for the Jansenist Christians—and here they are closer to the Middle Ages than they are to us—the miseries they felt and saw about them had also a grander dimension because they were a living symbol of man's beginning in Adam: man's present wickedness, and his incapacity to rise above his sins and avoid damnation argued his tainted inheritance of the concupiscence of Adam. Even man's awareness of his misery and his inadequate desires to reform were seen as a dim relic of Adam's former uprightness, and of the freedom and power he had once possessed to do God's will.

The enemies of Jansenism claimed that this 'reformation' was simply a revival of the heresies of Calvin: when the Jansenists exhorted the faithful to return to St Augustine and the 'Primitive Church' they were, in effect, mounting an attack upon the authority of the Church of Rome. Moreover, by destroying man's independence and free will, by making him totally dependent upon divine predestination, were they not making God himself responsible for everything man did, even for his most terrible sins? Yet it should be pointed out that these accusations simply ran roughshod over the careful distinctions and shadings of meaning giving Jansenism both its unique quality as literature and its validity as theology. On the contrary, the Jansenists argued that after the Fall, man retained a certain free will, through the efforts of which he could actually avoid any given sin at any given moment. And even though in avoiding one sin he would inevitably fall into another, he could at least conform to the accepted norms of human morality, as the apparently 'virtuous' lives of certain ancient pagans proved. Moreover, the Jansenists believed that all men always had the possibility of shunning sin, if they so willed; and even though at a given moment (*in sensu composito*) a man might find sin inevitable, there was a real possibility that, at another moment (*in sensu diviso*), sin might be avoided entirely.

Given the 'ineffable' depths of man's depravity, the idea of reproaching God for not having done more to save mankind was unthinkable. That He had done anything at all proved in itself the greatness of His mercy. And to be sure Christ had come to bestow grace upon those whom God in His infinite—if obscure—wisdom had chosen to save, and who, consequently, were given the power to rise above their sins and to perform acts of true virtue. Moreover—and here again Jansenism differs markedly from Calvinism —in addition to this grace granted to the elect, there were also other 'graces' either less intense, or of shorter duration (or both) that might impel a person to have faith, seek the good, or even to practise charity for a time, but that would then prove inadequate in some way and be withdrawn, leaving him to his sins and to God's just punishment for them. Finally, there is also the doctrine —unknown to Calvinism—that God occasionally saw fit to humble certain of the elect and make sure they sought their salvation in fear and trembling, by withdrawing temporarily His grace. St Peter, for example, had been chosen by God, and was eventually to be saved; however in order to make sure Peter realized how totally dependent he was upon God's mercy, God withdrew His grace for a time, and Peter could not help but thrice deny the Son of God.

One of the key elements in this theology was uncertainty: for even if one felt one had been chosen by God, one could never be sure that, the moment after, His grace might not be withdrawn, perhaps forever. And of course those who thought God had abandoned them were condemned to live out their existence floundering from one evil to another, seeing with terrible lucidity some of their sins, dimly aware that they must be committing others they did not even know. Even the sacraments might not bridge the gap: to Antoine Arnauld, Holy Communion was not a magical remedy for the sickness of the spirit. It was to strengthen and console those who were basically sound; and let no one dare approach the altar until, by prayer and fasting, he should have begun to advance along the way of contrition and penance. La mère Angélique, the great Abbesse of Port-Royal, whose noble face can be seen in the portraits by Philippe de Champaigne at Versailles and Chantilly, thought of herself, in God's sight, as 'a criminal at the stake, waiting for the Judge to execute His decree'. Even as death approached, she experienced agonies of mind in a long, spiritual purgatory: at the prospect of meeting her Maker, instead of peace and joy, the main emotion she felt was, quite simply, terror.

Jansenism spoke with many different voices; indeed it is astonishing to observe how the same doctrines can vary so radically in their tonality depending on who speaks them and the argument the speaker wishes to refute. And to be sure, the vast theological system of Jansenius proved mercifully elastic, allowing for many interpretations by those who sought to defend his Augustinianism. And yet, despite Arnauld's moving eloquence as he speaks—momentarily—of the abundance of God's grace for the elect, Noël de Lalane's efforts to stress the milder Thomist side of Jansenism, and Pierre Nicole's subtle dilution of the most austere of the *Pensées* of Pascal, the essence of Jansenism remains its severity. It was a movement of reform.

Jesuit Doctrines (Molinism)

As one turns from the Jansenists to certain of the seventeenth-century Jesuits, particularly to those who followed the celebrated Spanish Jesuit Luis de Molina, one senses immediately that the two 'sects' were made to be enemies of one another, and the feeling is borne out, to some extent, historically. For, even though Luis de Molina (1536—1609) died before the beginnings of Jansenism, his doctrine had been conceived directly in opposition to Thomists who invoked the authority of St Augustine; and, for his part, Jansenius had written specifically in order to refute Molina and his followers, such as Lessius, who were mainly Jesuits.[1]

If, for the Jansenists, sin and man's helplessness without grace formed the emotional centre of their belief, the Jesuits chose as a main point of reference the abundance of God's love and mercy, His eternally beneficent desires for all humanity. They insisted that the Jansenists were quite wrong to lay such stress upon the sins and guilt of mankind without taking these other truths sufficiently into account. To their mind, it was inconceivable that God should have left most of humanity without any real possibility of salvation; they denied that there was any fearsome design for all eternity tying mens' hands so they could not reach out towards grace. They rejected totally the idea that the stakes were down—at least in the Jansenist sense—even before men's lives were begun. They dismissed as impious the Jansenist belief that God might desert even those who strove with all they had to find Him. Gone are the dark nights of the soul, the salvations sought in fear and trembling, the desperately bleak view of man's lot; gone too are those piercing insights that seem to come only from the agonies of a mind and heart. Instead we have a smiling, more worldly sort of Christianity, far better suited to the courtly tastes of the time, whose central doctrines were undoubtedly both pious and moral, even though they sometimes became soft, perhaps a little rotten, when put into practice as ethics. Inheritors of the complicated traditions of scholasticism, the Jesuits had at their disposal endless sources of argument: proofs, 'distinctions', shadings of meaning, counter-truths, and loopholes for those who needed them.

Since God loved His creatures so much, the followers of Molina maintained that He had given all mankind the means of salvation through Christ and the Church. No one had been precluded in advance; a man had only to believe and repent, and

[1] On the differences between Molina and the later Molinists see Jan Miel, *Pascal and Theology* (Baltimore: The Johns Hopkins Press, 1970), pp. 50—53.

by countless means, both natural and supernatural, God was ceaselessly inviting him to do His will and be saved. This invitation and this possibility were called sufficient grace, *la grâce suffisante*. Through this grace, each person was endowed with the power to begin to believe in the true God, and to begin to love and serve Him (with the help of the Church and the sacraments, of course). No insurmountable obstacles in the mind or heart prevented man from obeying God: man, for example, had not been given a heart incapable of love; even original sin, an obstacle to be sure, could be overcome if man simply made the right choice—which indeed it was possible for him to do. In order to stress the reality of this possibility, the Molinists proposed that all men had the 'power' to do God's will, and because there was no barrier preventing this power from being put into effect (if man so willed) they called it 'proximate', *le pouvoir prochain*. Whenever man actually did avail himself of this power, thus eventually joining God's elect, it was said that 'sufficient' grace had become 'efficacious' grace, *la grâce efficace*.

The essence of these doctrines, indeed their whole object, is that they restored to man greater freedom of will. Again and again the Jesuits insisted on this point as they argued with the Jansenists. With their doctrine of *pouvoir prochain*, for example, they declared that this power must work in two directions, not only allowing man to accept God's grace, but enabling him, simultaneously, to reject it if he so willed. For if, as the Jansenists claimed, man were really not capable of rejecting God's grace at the moment it was proffered, if of necessity he was bound to do God's will, then clearly there was no 'merit' in his making the right choice; he literally did not deserve to be saved—nor, by the same token, would he deserve to be damned.

To give another example, the austere Jansenists often linked the concept of sin with the idea of 'blindness': man was so deeply sunk in his depravity, they said, he could not even see the whole extent of his sinfulness; indeed he was committing a number of sins—and quite rightly punished by God for them—without even being aware of their existence. But the Jesuits would not tolerate such terrors of darkness. They argued that for an act to be counted against someone as a sin, the person must have some possibility of making a different choice: what parent would be so cruel as to punish a child for misbehaving when the child literally didn't know he was doing wrong, or couldn't possibly have behaved otherwise? If a man were starving, what judge would be so heartless as to condemn him to eternal torment simply because he had not realised that the food he so desperately devoured was bacon and that the season was Lent? To the Jesuits it was clear that for an act to be counted as a sin, the doer had to be aware of the evil nature of the deed, and possess the power to avoid the sin, if he wanted to. Again they stated that this power was 'proximate' (*le pouvoir prochain*), and it should be regarded as a kind of outgrowth of 'sufficient' grace: even when sunk to the lowest depths of his wickedness, man always had the power to do God's will, if he wanted to, for God never abandoned him entirely. Although He had given man the freedom to reject as well as to accept His divine will, He constantly and eternally desired the salvation of everyone, provided they would obey Him. Such was the meaning of Christ's coming.

The Jesuits placed great reliance upon the power of the sacraments, while at the same time accusing the Jansenists of underestimating their importance. For example, it seemed to the Jesuits that their opponents were forever moaning about the disastrous consequences of Adam's sin, without realising the Baptism had been instituted precisely in order to wash away the most harmful of these effects: the original disaster had been reduced to a present misfortune. Men had other sacraments at their disposal also, in time of need: for those in poor spiritual health they often recommended frequent communion. Was it reasonable to deny the warmth of the fire to those who were perishing of cold? The sacrament of Penance was likewise considered beneficial, especially to those who could not summon a feeling of repentance. For the Jesuits knew very well that true repentance—the painful descent to humility in the consciousness of sin, the burning desire and the earnest intent to reform the heart and mind, called 'contrition'—was extremely difficult for most persons to achieve. No doubt if they truly loved God, as they should, they would feel contrite. But the fact was, the Jesuits candidly recognized, that many persons simply did not love God to this degree. And rather than refuse such persons absolution—as the Jansenists recommended—a number of Jesuits declared that if a man were frightened at the prospect of eternal torment, and perhaps also sincerely regretted he could not feel a deeper repentance, he might be granted absolution for this simple 'attrition'. There was hope that, fortified by the sacrament, he might be better enabled to achieve the sought-for change of heart. It was in this spirit also that they viewed the famous problem of the 'necessity' of loving God. In short, whereas to the Jansenists the sacraments of Communion and Penance were often thought of as confirmations of a spiritual regeneration that was already underway, the Jesuits regarded them also as the means by which this regeneration might be initiated.

It is tempting to yield to the impression that in the religion of the Jesuits the outward and visible is replacing entirely the inward and spiritual: they seem forever ready to accept a facile lip-service in place of those harder-won virtues that come from the heart. Because of their reliance upon the inherent strength of ritual formula, their stress on ceremonial, and their sometimes indiscriminate promotion of miracles, relics, statues of saints, the cult of the Virgin Mary, medals, feast days, and pilgrimages, they were the prime target of the Calvinists in their attacks on Popish superstition. Yet if one looks at the theological doctrines behind these outward prescriptions, it is clear that such beliefs and practices, however abusive they may have become, have something more to be said in their favour than their enemies cared to admit. The heart of the matter is, once again, the relationship between 'sufficient' grace and 'efficacious' grace. This is to say that the central issue is whether or not a man really does have the power to take advantage of Christ's sacrifice and be saved. As we have seen, the Jesuits thought that man did have this power: <u>that man, by his own free will (and with God's help) could turn the</u>

possibility of salvation offered through 'sufficient' grace into the reality which was 'efficacious' grace. The Jansenists, on the other hand, believed that man did not have this power: even though the merit of Christ's sacrifice was infinite, man could never really take advantage of it, unless God—entirely according to His own inscrutable will—chose to send him a special, irresistible grace which would save him.

Looking now at the consequences of these doctrines in terms of devotional practices, Jansenists such as Arnauld believed that a man who found himself in a state of sin had no power whatsoever to change his empty, fruitless gestures into heartfelt expressions of piety: he might get down on his knees, but he could not even pray sincerely for help without some form of God's grace. To participate in the ceremonies, to take the sacraments of the Church while in such a state, was at best useless and at worst a profanation of holy things. For the Jesuits, the contrary was true: man indeed possessed the power to vivify his empty gestures and work his salvation if he so willed; in fact, to go through the motions of piety might actually help to induce a truly religious feeling in man's stony heart. Since salvation was the result of spontaneous cooperation between God and man, the Church's role was to provide numerous invitations to man so that he might make a beginning. No token was considered too small, no action too vain; for everything was potentially a promise of greater spiritual advancement, and a symbol of the time when man might actually use his proximate power to make God's 'sufficient' grace at last 'efficacious'.

Considering the controversy in a purely secular manner, it might seem a paradox that the Jansenists, while choosing a God of whom they asked relatively little, a God who doled out salvation with an eye-dropper; withdrawn, often apparently indifferent to human suffering, obscure of motive, and virtually unfindable to man's reason, should at the same time demand so very much of themselves in love of God, purity of heart and the practice of the austerest virtue. The reverse was true for the Jesuits: their God was supposed to do far more for humanity. He was more loving, compassionate, merciful, accessible to man's reason; and He was always available when sought to give man aid. Yet at the same time they required far less of themselves in terms of ethics, or even in terms of devotion. This generalization does not hold for all. There were numerous Jesuits in the seventeenth century whose morals were austere enough to have satisfied the Bishop of Hippo, as well as Jansenists who did not practise their principles. Yet the Jansenist approach to ethics, which simply by-passed most of the medieval scholastic tradition in order to concentrate on the doctrines of the 'Primitive Church' represented both an intellectual simplification of the problem, and at the same time an emotional intensification in regard to it. To the Jansenists, the kind of virtue demanded by St Augustine seemed not only clear but even simple in its uncompromising purity. Virtue, like truth, seemed one. And somehow the more conscious they were of the great load of sin weighing them down, of the abyss yawning between them and God, the more ardently they yearned and strained to reach this perfection.

The Jesuits on the other hand saw themselves as inheritors of the whole continuity of the Church's ethical traditions, and, in their view, ethical doctrines must adapt themselves as men developed and society changed. They willingly conceded that St Augustine was in many ways an excellent model, but they pointed out that one hardly could expect him to have anticipated every ethical problem that would arise in the following one thousand years; nor was he infallible on every point, for a number of his contemporaries and predecessors, equally revered for their piety, had not always taken the same view as he. In short, the Jesuits believed that in ethical matters the Moderns were quite as sagacious as the Ancients: the Church was still the Church of Christ, and its priests were still sure guides, perhaps even surer than those of times past, for the Church was now more ancient and hence more wise.

Since ethical truth, in the eyes of the Jesuits, was linked to man's changing conditions and also to the changing needs of the Church, such truth was essentially complex, and a single moral problem might admit of numerous solutions, each having various degrees of probability. This was why the Jesuits developed the subtle art of casuistry to an extent that went far beyond the Jansenists, who were content with simpler methods. Nor were the Jesuits impressed with the austerities of the followers of St Augustine. On the contrary, they considered the 'angelic' purity preached by their opponents to be quite literally inhuman; impossible to attain for most, it was destined simply to make men despair and drive them from religion. The Jesuits also pointed out the ironic contradiction in Jansenism, that all the while these purists were pointing accusing fingers at sinners, threatening eternal torments if they would not repent, their theory of predestination saw to it that virtually no one could comply.

Here is one Jesuit view, expressed, some years before the 'Provincial Letters', by Father Brisacier, S.J.:

> Les Hérésies les plus dangereuses ne font jamais aucun progrès, que sous prétexte de réforme et sous l'apparence de piété [. . .]: quand un visage pâle, maigre et défiguré montre le blanc des yeux avec un tordion de tête, et que mêlant deux ou trois soupirs, il a dit que la ferveur du Christianisme est ralentie, qu'on ne vit plus dans l'innocence du Baptême, que le lustre de l'Eglise primitive est terni, qu'il la faut ramener dans son ancienne forme et renouveler la vertu, et, qu'avec une mine austère il a blâmé les abus, parlé de réforme, et montré quelque austérité dans sa vie [. . .] *Prenez garde aux faux Prophètes. (Le Jansénisme confondu . . .* (Paris, 1651), p. 31.)

As Monsieur Gazier suggested long ago, Jansenism and the religion of the Jesuits gave expression to two different ways of *being*. Sometimes this is true in a curiously literal way: the Jansenists generally preferred to think of themselves as physically thin, for example, while the Jesuits were willing to tolerate more *embonpoint*. (Molière's Tartuffe with 'le teint frais, et la bouche vermeille' conveys the popular idea of this perfectly.) Jansenist prose style at its best was not only elegant, but had a certain spare quality, 'un style nerveux' the French would say, 'masculine eloquence' Gilbert Burnet called it. Jesuit prose style, on the other hand, was typically more ornamental, sometimes even flowery; and, like the architecture of their churches, we associate it more readily with the idea of 'baroque'.[1] Professor Bénichou points out that Jansenism, with its almost self-righteous stress on the importance of virtue, fits better with a middle-class mentality, while the religion of the Jesuits, with its elaborate casuistry minimizing the penalties for such things as duelling, private vengeance, amorous exploits, and over-indulgence, tended rather to support the traditional aristocracy.[2] It was particularly relevant, as Professor Gilbert Gadoffre has suggested, to the military caste.

Jansenism appealed most strongly to people who wanted to question matters, and perhaps that statement summarizes most of the reasons why it caused such trouble, and excitement, in seventeenth-century France. Partly because the systematic doubt of Cartesian philosophy coincided so well with this attitude, Descartes was welcomed in Port-Royal—at Aristotle's expense, and also somewhat at that of certain religious doctrines formerly supported by aristotelian arguments. Naturally the Jansenists would not hear of sacrificing the philosophical truths of Descartes for mere expediency; the theologians and philosophers would simply have to devise a new set of Cartesian proofs to make the same points. And yet—as in the famous case of the Transubstantiation—this was not always so easily done as they might wish. The structure seemed actually to strain, while the watchful Jesuits, loyal to Aristotle, reported loudly on every crack they could find ... The example is not the only one of its kind, and perhaps the opponents of Jansenism were justified in their scepticism whenever these Augustinians tried to minimize the consequences of their reforms. For on the contrary, implied in Jansenism were transformations of the whole nature of Catholic-

[1] See Jean Marmier, 'Les Provinciales, Œuvre anti-baroque' in *Mélanges d'histoire littéraire (XVIe—XVIIe siècle)* offerts à Raymond Lebegue ... (Paris: Nizet, 1969).

[2] *Morales du grand siècle* (Paris: Gallimard, 1948), and H.W.S. Baird, *Studies in Pascal's Ethics* (The Hegne = Nijhoff, 1975), p. 39ff.

ism. Nor did it stop there, for if one considers the forces at work in the Jansenist movement, its political context seems quite as important as its religious implications.

The Jansenist Movement from Richelieu's Oppression to the Release of Saint-Cyran (1638–1643)

Part of the importance of the *Provinciales* is that they reflect with such intensity a particular moment in French religious history; they are, in the best sense of the term, occasional pieces, belonging to the same tradition as the *Satyre ménipée*, the *Lettres persanes* of Montesquieu, and the *Lettres philosophiques* of Voltaire. In our simplified modern perspective, the occasions giving birth to Pascal's *Lettres* seem very complex. Perhaps this impression is inevitable, given the nature of the Jansenist movement.[1]

Jansenism had its beginning in France under the oppressive rule of Cardinal de Richelieu—hardly an auspicious moment, one might think, for the start of a religious reform. Yet, the strength of conviction of the early adherents to Jansenism is awesome; their suffering seemed only to endow them with greatness—nor, indeed, was there any lack of opponents willing to inflict punishments upon them.

Richelieu's main quarrel with the Jansenists—particularly with Saint-Cyran—concerned their rigid doctrine of 'contrition' in the sacrament of Penance: contrary to the Jesuits, the Jansenists would not agree that merely wishing one could feel sorrier than one actually did, or fearing one would be punished later in hell, or some sort of watery incipient regret (known as 'attrition') would be sufficient to earn God's approval; true repentance was something more fundamental. It is interesting to consider why Richelieu was so hostile towards the Jansenists on this point. Contemporary accounts give two answers: the Jansenist, Godefroi

---

[1]See R. Taveneaux, *Jansénisme et Politique* (Paris: Colin, 1965) and Antoine Adam, *Du Mysticisme à la révolte, les Jansénistes du XVIIe siècle* (Paris: Fayard, 1968).

Hermant, claimed that Richelieu himself was beset by secret fears
that he did not feel sorry enough for his own innumerable sins. He
needed reassurance, and could not bear the sight of those who, in
doctrine, seemed to be pointing guilty fingers at him. Other
contemporaries maintained that it was King Louis XIII who,
pious and somewhat weak-willed, was concerned that his feelings
of repentance might not be deep enough. If this version is the
true one, Richelieu certainly did whatever he could to allay the
King's fears: he firmly supported the sufficiency of attrition himself, and he saw to it that the King's confessors were Jesuits who
agreed with his view. Historians relate that there were a variety of
reasons—including reasons of foreign policy—why Richelieu
might have distrusted Saint-Cyran, but perhaps it was above all
because Richelieu's own ascendancy over the King was involved
that, when an Oratorian by the name of Séguenot published a
work, *De la sainte Virginité*, which seemed to support the Jansenist
idea of contrition, and Richelieu's informants told him that the
work had actually been inspired by Saint-Cyran, the Cardinal
took the extreme measure of having both Séguenot and the Abbé
de Saint-Cyran sent to prison (14 May 1638).

This was one of the most difficult moments French Jansenism
would ever have to endure. Jansenius himself had died just a few
days before (6 May 1638), and now, with the imprisonment of
Saint-Cyran, the Abbey of Port-Royal would be deprived of its
principal spiritual director for more than three and a half years.
(Saint-Cyran only survived for nine months after his release from
Vincennes prison.) The 'solitaires' of Port-Royal dispersed and the
Sorbonne, at Richelieu's request, condemned Séguenot's book,
and thus in effect condemned Saint-Cyran's doctrine of contrition (1 June 1638). A series of investigations and interrogations
harassed Saint-Cyran, and made his friends fear for his safety.[1]

Meanwhile, almost predictably, the Jesuits seemed to be
flourishing everywhere in this period from 1638 to 1642: Father
Bauny, a professor at the Jesuits' Collège de Clermont in Paris,

[1] Partly responsible for initiating these investigations was Pierre Séguier who, as Chancellor,
was to become the most powerful legal figure in France.

published several works at this time that went as far in 'moral laxism' as any French Jesuit would dare to go in his century; Father Cellot, S.J., concentrated his efforts in print on reforming the Church hierarchy: in his view it was time to diminish the authority of bishops—to the profit of Rome and the Jesuits, naturally enough. Father Antoine Sirmond, S.J., confronted with the question of whether one was required to love God, so diluted this obligation that anyone who took his advice seriously learned forthwith not to worry about it; the helpful ally of the Jesuits, the wise and witty La Mothe le Vayer, expanded the importance of the natural virtues so much—while at the time appropriately diminishing the role of Redemption—that he seemed ready to save all the heathen in the remotest jungles, provided they show an ounce of good will (*De la Vertu des payens*, 1642).

There were protests, indeed a remarkable number of them, considering Richelieu's almost protective attitude towards the Jesuits and the dread he inspired. The Assemblée du clergé de France courageously issued a formal condemnation of the works by the Jesuits Bauny and Cellot. Most surprisingly, they ordered a reprinting of certain works written by the imprisoned Abbé de Saint-Cyran, works which he had composed earlier and published under an assumed name. Because Saint-Cyran had supported the authority of bishops, the Assemblée was convinced that the reprinting would serve as a useful antidote to Father Cellot and his ilk. Yet such efforts were largely fruitless: Richelieu saw to it that the condemnation of Father Bauny was never published so long as the Jesuit survived. As for the fresh edition of the works by Saint-Cyran (published under the pseudonym 'Petrus Aurelius'), the formidable Chancellor of France, Séguier, simply absconded with all the copies as soon as they were printed, and even later, after Louis XIII's death, he refused to surrender them when formally requested to do so by the Assemblée du clergé. The pattern of events recurred when, in November 1640, the Sorbonne set up a commission to examine the ethical doctrines of Father Bauny: Richelieu blocked them from taking any action, and again it was Chancellor Séguier who conveyed his order to the Sorbonne (1 August 1641). On the other hand, Richelieu had made up his mind that the Faculty of Theology was going to examine the doctrines of Jansenius and condemn them; the theologian Habert would preach sermons against the *Augustinus*, and Alphonse Lemoine would refute Jansenius in a course of lectures in the Sorbonne.

Trouble was also to come from Rome. Already at the time of the publication of the *Augustinus* Pope Urban VIII had issued a decree prohibiting this work. In 1641, on the very same day that the Chancellor conveyed Richelieu's orders to the Sorbonne, the Holy Office in Rome published another decree prohibiting, provisionally, the *Augustinus*, and everything written for or against it. In March, 1642, there came the first of the Papal Bulls against Jansenius. This Bull, 'In Eminenti', was not officially promulgated until later, but its existence already in early 1642 gives an indication of the way the wind was going to blow from that quarter.

The Jansenists in France meanwhile bided their time, publishing almost nothing, but working industriously behind the scenes to gain partisans and allies. Richelieu's oppression actually strengthened their determination: all the works published by the Jesuits favouring free will and diluting the severity of penance simply made the Jansenists see all the more clearly the necessity for their reforms. As for the imprisonment of Saint-Cyran, it would not be the first time, they said, that a Christian had been persecuted unjustly for believing the truth. The nuns at Port-Royal remained loyal to their imprisoned spiritual director; the 'solitaires' were ready to reassemble; Antoine Arnauld was only waiting for the chance to publish.

Looking at the events today, one wonders how the Jansenists could have been so confident that their time would come. As it was, their short-lived period of triumph was due to an historical accident which might easily have been delayed: Richelieu died on 4 December 1642, and with his demise the wheel of fortune turned in their favour. Saint-Cyran was liberated from prison (6 February 1643). Then King Louis XIII died (14 May 1643), and Cardinal

Mazarin, coming into power as prime minister, was reluctant to get very deeply involved in the Jansenist quarrel.[1] So at last the moment had arrived for the Jansenists to speak out, and, in August 1643, Arnauld's treatise *De la fréquente Communion* appeared bearing the approbation of sixteen bishops or archbishops and twenty doctors of theology. It was to be, along with Pascal's *Provinciales* and the *Essais de Morale* by Pierre Nicole, one of the most influential works of theology ever written by a Jansenist. At approximately the same date Arnauld published, in collaboration with Hallier, *La Théologie morale des Jésuites*, laying the groundwork for a number of Pascal's arguments and souring the dispositions of Jesuit polemicists for the rest of the century. Arnauld was at last awarded the title of 'socius' in the Sorbonne, a promotion he had sought in vain so long as Richelieu was alive.

The Jansenists might have taken some comfort from the funeral rites for the Abbé de Saint-Cyran held on 12 October 1643. They were celebrated by three bishops; assisting at the ceremonies were the Bishop of Amiens, the Archbishop of Bordeaux, the Bishops of Valence, Calcedonia and Aire, the Coadjutor of Montauban, as well as numerous persons of quality. (We find these facts noted scrupulously, and somewhat in the manner of the cat watching the mice at play, in the *Mémoires* of Father Rapin, a Jesuit.) One month later, on 29 November 1643, the bishops assembled at Mazarin's *hôtel* solemnly condemned Father Nouet, S.J., for his sermons attacking Arnauld's recent treatise on communion. Because he had offended the bishops approving Arnauld's work, they declared that the Jesuit must openly retract what he had said, in a posture of humility, on his knees.

Jansenism and French Institutions

The French Jansenists had certainly survived their first crisis with success; the Assemblée du clergé, the Sorbonne, the Paris Parlement all seemed to be smiling upon them. The Archbishop of

[1] Cf. Paule Jansen, *Le Cardinal Mazarin et le mouvement janséniste français* (Paris: Vrin, 1967).

Toulouse, whose thundering eloquence could sway the entire Assemblée du clergé when he spoke, was on their side; aristocratic persons such as the Duc de Luynes were known to be supporting them; Arnauld's theological works, composed largely in French rather than in Latin, reached a wide public and seemed to be winning friends everywhere. And yet, despite such undoubted accomplishments, their triumph was partly an illusion, and one would do well to scrutinize it rather carefully. For no matter how many votes were cast in their favour by the Sorbonne and the Assemblée du clergé, the fact remains that the severe doctrines of the Jansenists probably never commanded a true majority in either of these institutions, which is to say that most of the French Church would not accept the Jansenist view of sin, predestination and grace. The movement remained everywhere a minority phenomenon, indeed part of the Jansenists' strength lay in their being 'the little flock', for whom vigilance was a prime necessity, and who had to struggle unremittingly in order not to be submerged. Nor should one forget the nature of their adversaries: in the period under consideration, from Saint-Cyran's incarceration to the publication of the *Provinciales*, the Jansenists had to undergo the intermittent hostilities of two of the King's prime ministers, a whole series of royal confessors, the Chancellor, the King's Council, the Queen-Mother, several popes, and the Roman Curia; Louis XIV, whose '*sacre*' at Rheims took place in 1654, willingly followed suit.

The Assemblée du clergé and the Sorbonne would soon prove fickle friends for the Jansenists; the Parlement, often occupied by more pressing matters such as the Fronde revolt, was not supposed to meddle in theology more than legally necessary. The sixteen approbations from bishops for Arnauld's treatise on communion in 1643 may seem a remarkable achievement; on the other hand their opponents, less than a decade later, easily obtained more than sixty signatures from bishops in order to have the famous 'five points', allegedly taken from the *Augustinus*, 'examined' by the Pope. To be sure, the elements of the problem were different. Some bishops undoubtedly changed sides during the intervening period, and a few others protested, a little lamely, that asking for an examination was not equivalent to asking the Pope to condemn the work; but even so, in most cases the request was a sign of hostility towards Jansenism, and such a large number as this virtually eliminates the possibility that the Jansenists ever had anything like a majority of the bishops favourable to their views.

The key to their success probably lay less in the edifying austerity of their doctrines, or even in their energetic dedication to religious reform than in the overlapping of their movement with other established causes that brought them a certain transitory popularity. The clearest example was their campaign against the Jesuits: to be sure, it had grown directly and most logically from their own theological position. On the other hand, they were far from being the originators of belligerence against the Company of Jesus; indeed, the Jesuits had met opposition from many quarters in France ever since the middle of the sixteenth century when they first tried to establish an educational institution in Paris.

Three sources of Anti-Jesuit support for the Jansenits

(1) The Paris Parlement
Parlement had led the fight to keep the Jesuits out: in 1551, and again in 1553, it refused to register the Letters patent of Henri II which would have let them set up a college in the capital. In 1560, under François II, Parlement on two occasions refused to accept similar Letters, and the delegates continued to argue and balk until 1562, when they gave in, having been assured that the Jesuits would be severely restricted: it was stated that they would not even be allowed to use the word 'Jesuit' in the name of their institution, which would be called 'Le Collège de Clermont'. When it turned out that a would-be assassin of Henri IV, Chatel, had been studying at the Collège de Clermont just before he made his attempt on the King's life, Parlement again led the successful fight to have the Jesuits expelled from France (1594), and it was in spite of Parlement's bitter opposition that Henri IV allowed them to return from exile in 1603. Nor would Parlement

agree to register any Letters patent enabling the Jesuits to reopen the detested Collège de Clermont for more than a decade after their return.

Such passionate hatred as this on the part of the Paris Parlement, showing itself in the century of France's religious wars and continuing, intermittently, for two whole centuries, is a very curious and complex phenomenon, and we cannot hope here to probe deeply into the reasons behind it. Yet we can note, in a more general way, that the quarrel between the Jesuits and Parlement has an element of a social conflict: the Jesuits' Collège de Clermont in the rue St Jacques, though open to all classes (even to sons of *parlementaires*), quickly became an aristocratic centre, richly endowed, and the list of its students includes some from the great houses of France. The delegates to Parlement, on the other hand, were comparatively strait-laced members of the legal caste, and they were continually calling the Jesuits to account, trying to keep them out of positions of power, denouncing their immoral teachings, demanding that they obey the rules and conform to more rigid standards—just like the good bourgeois that these delegates often were.

We may observe also, without trying to push the matter too far, that their hostility towards the Jesuits brought Parlement again and again into real opposition to the crown. One of Parlement's main objections to the Jesuits was the special oath they swore pledging faithfulness to the Pope. The Parlement was convinced that this loyalty to Rome was incompatible with loyalty to the King of France: they pointed to the disloyal conduct of certain Jesuits at the time of the Ligue and there were too many writings by Jesuits, particularly in Spain and Italy, which proved in cold print that they believed in the permissibility of regicide—under certain conditions—to be dismissed easily. The delegates to Parlement tried repeatedly to persuade the King to oppose the Jesuits if only for his own personal safety, not to mention the well-being of the realm. Yet, with the possible exception of Henri IV, it is fair to say that none of the rulers of France up to the time of the young Louis XIV took their warnings seriously. On the contrary, it became traditional for the King's confessor to be chosen *always* from among the Jesuits. We may conclude that the Parlement was asking the crown to participate in a spirit of independence from Papal authority, of bourgeois morality and bourgeois 'nationalism' (for want of a better term) which, when asserted in the form of policies against the Jesuits, the crown instinctively felt was alien to itself.

'Les Libertés de l'Église gallicane' was the key phrase in this connection, and everyone, from the King and Parlement to the Assemblée du clergé and the Sorbonne, agreed that these liberties did exist (they were quite commonly traced back to Charlemagne) and that they must be protected.[1] At the same time, there were rather wide differences of opinion concerning their nature and extent, and the means one should employ to guard them. Some Jesuits seemed to think that the best way to protect these liberties was to show obedience to Rome: the Church was one, and the Holy Father had the French Church's own interests at heart, hence in this case, service was perfect freedom.

(2) The bishops of the Assemblée du clergé
To most of the bishops and *curés* of the Assemblée du clergé de France, on the other hand, the greatest bastion of Gallican liberties was the strength of the 'secular' clergy, i.e. of the Bishops and *curés* themselves. They of course recognized the primacy of the Bishop of Rome, yet, at the same time, they were determined that they should have a measure of independence, and many of them preferred to think of the Church hierarchy as being less of an absolute monarchy under the rule of the Pope than a sort of joint monarchy and aristocracy, rather vaguely combined. It was in this spirit that the Assemblée du clergé set about protecting the French episcopacy against encroachments.

The bishops were convinced that, historically, the main villains of the piece were the Jesuits, who seemed forever to be

[1] See William Bouwsma, *Gallicanism and the Nature of Christendom* in Anthony Molho and John A. Tedeschi, eds., *Renaissance Studies in Honor of Hans Baron* (Florence, 1971), pp. 811—830.

nibbling away at episcopal authority: preaching unauthorized sermons in the diocese, illegally establishing educational institutions, publishing immoral or—worse still—anti-episcopal works, challenging the right of the Assemblée du clergé to discipline them. The most flagrant case had involved England: although earlier in the seventeenth century the Jesuits had taken a leading role in the clandestine practice of Roman Catholicism in England (they functioned under the authority of a Dean and Chapter), in 1625, the Pope sent the Bishop of Calcedonia to England to organize the hierarchy. Jesuit resentment of this intrusion was immediate. They attacked the bishop in their writings, some even composed treatises arguing against the extended authority of bishops: religious orders had done well enough until then without the interference of a bishop, and they would be better off without one in the future.

These were the Jesuits originally challenged by the Abbé de Saint-Cyran in the works which the Assemblée du clergé insisted on reprinting while the Abbé was still in prison under Richelieu, and perhaps the issue of the liberties of the Gallican Church best explains why the prelates showed such dogged determination in seeing that these refutations actually reached the bookseller: after Chancellor Séguier had refused to surrender the copies he had taken under the late King Louis XIII, the prelates then voted fresh funds for a new reprinting, which was duly brought forth to the public. Saint-Cyran's support of the episcopacy seems entirely consistent with the general tendency of Jansenism to shift the emphasis away from Rome, which in turn grew from their desire to recapture the style of the 'Primitive Church'. At the same time it won them votes from prelates who might not otherwise have looked so favourably upon them.

Theoretically, the Assemblée du clergé confined its discussions to matters of discipline and finance; it did not rule on matters of doctrine, which were the province of the Sorbonne. In reality, however, the Assemblée du clergé found it impossible to draw the line between discipline and doctrine, and one frequently finds the prelates of the Assemblée and the Doctors of the Sorbonne ruling upon the same issues. In regard to the Company of Jesus, they often took similar stands, the Sorbonne having many reasons also to dislike the Jesuits. Here too the quarrel went back many years, and in part the attitude of the Sorbonne reflected that of the University of Paris as a whole.

(3) The University of Paris

Insofar as the University of Paris was a religious institution, it belonged essentially to the 'secular' clergy—as distinguished from the 'regular' clergy, vulgarly referred to as the 'monks'. Members of religious orders were strictly limited in their participation in the University, and the Rector was supposed to be ever watchful in enforcing the rules. Since the University had already been working to keep the 'monks' in their place for centuries, the appearance of the Jesuits on the scene merely presented a new version of a very old problem. To be sure, the Jesuits were not 'monks' in the ordinary sense of the word, because, although they took vows and obeyed a 'rule' as all the regular clergy did, at the same time their style of living and even their dress, was modelled after the priests of the secular clergy. Unfortunately for them, all this ambiguity accomplished was to earn them the epithet 'hermaphrodites' from the unkindest of their adversaries. The University resolutely grouped them with the 'monks' and proceeded accordingly: like the Paris Parlement, the University fought to keep the Jesuits from opening the Collège de Clermont in the rue St Jacques, and though they lost that battle, at least they somehow managed—despite a ruling to the contrary by the Privy Council—to enforce a stipulation that no student should be given his degree from the regular Faculty of Arts, or Theology, if he was known to have taken courses from the Jesuits. And they won several smaller battles: they kept the Jesuits from teaching in such places as Senlis and Pontoise, and they resisted much of the pressure exerted upon them to admit the Collège de Clermont as part of the University or to accept the Jesuit curriculum as being equivalent to their own.

The reason for the University's firmness in this matter was

partly their traditional policy that the 'monks' should generally be restricted to the education of those who, like themselves, intended to take vows. But in the case of the Collège de Clermont one suspects there may also have been a factor of jealousy: while several of the other colleges of the University were in a state of dilapidation and disrepair, languishing for want of students, competent masters, and, above all, funds, the Collège de Clermont was actually thriving: they were so wealthy that they wanted to offer their courses gratis, which (had the other faculties seen fit to permit it) would have drained students from every part of the University. As it was the students attended in droves: Richelieu helped the Jesuits to take over the adjoining Collège de Marmoutiers in order to expand their facilities. It became a favourite institution for the sons of the aristocracy. Louis XIV was especially partial to the Collège de Clermont, which was why the Jesuits later changed its name to 'Louis-le-grand'.

The Sorbonne

For its part, the Faculty of Theology of the University, the Sorbonne, also had much experience in the difficult art of keeping the 'monks' in their place, and the struggle continued until almost literally the eve of the first *Provinciale*. Legally, each of the four mendicant orders occupying 'houses' in Paris had, originally in 1552, been allotted just two votes in the Sorbonne. In 1598, this number was increased to five Dominicans, four Franciscans, three Augustinians and three Carmelites, and after this the number apparently continued to grow simply through laxity in applying the regulations. But in 1626 the issue exploded over the efforts of the Sorbonne to maintain its previous censure of an Italian Jesuit, Santarelli, who had exalted the power of the Pope above that of the kings, thus enraging the Gallicans. It was well known that the mendicant orders almost invariably sided with Rome and the Jesuits, and the vote in the Sorbonne was so close that if the mendicants were not pared down to something like their original number, the previous vote of censure—taken when most of the mendicants were conveniently absent—might be reversed.

The alignment of forces was the usual one, whenever the Jesuits were involved: The Paris Parlement was the most vehement in its determination to maintain the censure and restrict the 'monks' legally to the minimum number of votes. The Faculty of Theology was also generally quite firm in its desire to hold to the censure, despite such theologians as Duval, who were organizing the opposition. On the other hand, the Papal Nuncio in Paris, realizing that the crisis involved Papal supremacy, the fate of the Jesuits in France, and perhaps also the permanent voting character of the Sorbonne, worked energetically behind the scenes to have the censure reversed or annulled. He was seconded by Cardinal de Bérulle, who was a skilful negotiator, but his trump card was the King's Council of State which came out on his side: in the last analysis the crown did not wish to see either the Jesuits punished, or the mendicants' influence in the Faculty of Theology impaired, or, above all, to have the question of the King's sovereignty—as opposed to that of the Papacy—ventilated in the Sorbonne and Parlement.

After it became clear that all the back-stage manoeuvering by the Nuncio, Richelieu, and the Duvalist faction would be inadequate to stem the violent feelings aroused by these issues, the King himself intervened, declaring that henceforth there was to be no discussion of anything connected with Santarelli's 'detestable' doctrines because he was reserving for himself the right to settle the problem, in good time. There were very angry protests against this intervention in the Sorbonne, and they only began to subside when Richelieu, in the King's name, issued a veiled threat of reprisal against the troublemakers. Parlement too was incensed, and it would not give way until Louis XIII summoned the Presiding Judge into his presence and commanded him to see that Parlement obeyed, which it finally did on 3 February 1627. Thus the censure of Santarelli's doctrine on Papal authority was not allowed official sanction, the Gallicans in the Sorbonne were not supported by the crown, and the number of 'monks' voting in the Sorbonne was not reduced to its original size.

Gallicans against the Papacy

The idea of Papal authority in this period has, traditionally, something so solemn about it, that we are surprised to find the Pope's own representative in Paris, the Nuncio, rushing about with rather undignified haste, trying to scrape up a few more votes in the Faculty of Theology, or to read that Richelieu, in a pet over Rome's blunders in the Santarelli affair, had refused for a time even to grant the Nuncio an audience. There was also a surprising amount of doctrinal independence from Rome: although the Council of Trent had been the most significant Church council of modern times, its decisions were never officially in force in France, because the Third Estate, seconded by the Paris Parlement, had vigorously opposed recognition in 1615. Papal Bulls had no real authority in France unless they were 'received', 'registered' by the Parlement, and also 'published' and inscribed in the registers of the Faculty of Theology—and this was far from being a mere formality: the first Papal Bull against the *Augustinus*, for example, was not fully accepted in the official sense by the Sorbonne, despite much agitation by the Nuncio. It was also opposed by the Paris Parlement. The Sorbonne was quite capable, as the Santarelli affair showed, of condemning a work that had been approved in Rome; nor was Rome's Index of prohibited books necessarily binding upon French Christians, because the Sorbonne—along with the Chancellor who had the power to grant, or deny, his privilege for the legal publication of books— preferred to regulate such matters itself. The Nuncio had to stand by and see the *Augustinus* reprinted in Paris, despite Papal prohibition; moreover the copies bore approbations from six Doctors of the Sorbonne. The Inquisition, the terror of Spain and Italy, was not allowed in France largely because the Sorbonne, and above all Parlement, would not permit it.

One might wonder why the Papacy was willing to tolerate a state of affairs so humiliating to itself, and why the Popes did not bring the Gallicans into line by applying more forceful measures such as they had successfully done in other Latin countries. One of the most interesting answers to this question is suggested in a letter written by the Papal Nuncio, Spada, to Richelieu during the Santarelli affair. The Nuncio was worried because the situation was getting out of hand in the Sorbonne, while Richelieu did little but sulk:

> Monseigneur Illustrissime. Nous sommes dans le pire gouffre où nous ayons jamais été et nous voici à la veille d'un schisme; nous voici au serment d'Angleterre,[1] et si V[otre] S[eigneur] ie Ill [ustrissi]me n'y met la main et ne prend nettement position, si le remède ne s'administre pas avant demain matin, il sera trop tard . . . [3 April 1626, Bib. nat., ital. 64, f. 28, quoted in Martin, *Le Gallicanisme politique*, p. 197.]

One occasionally forgets how much the history of the sixteenth-century Reformation weighed upon the Catholic Church of the seventeenth. But of course, despite an outward appearance of serene indifference, the mere knowledge that most of Northern Europe had turned against Catholicism was a continually sobering lesson for Rome. If the Papacy did not apply more direct pressure on France, it was because some Gallicans appeared to be only waiting for an excuse to cut all ties with the Pope. In short, there seemed a real possibility that if tempers in the Sorbonne and Parlement did not cool off, and if the Papacy cracked the whip, thus adding fresh sources of irritation from the outside, the French Church might go the way of England.

The Tide turns against the Jansenists. The Controversy of the 'Five Points'

Despite great effort by the Jansenists to disguise the truth from themselves, and despite also a curious lack of decisiveness on the part of Rome, it is clear from the development of the facts that Rome was generally hostile to the Jansenists throughout this period. By June 1643 there had been two decrees of the Holy Office and a Papal Bull against the *Augustinus*. At the end of

[1] The reference here is to the Oath of Supremacy imposed in 1606 by James I.

July 1644 there came still another decree of the Holy Office attesting to the authenticity of the Bull, which the Jansenists had been calling a forgery. Unfortunately for Rome, the moment for issuing the decree was, to say the least, badly chosen, since its date coincided exactly with that of the death of Urban VIII, the Pope responsible for the Bull in the first place. The Jansenists continued to cry 'fraud' and would refuse to see the obvious truth that the Pope—or at least those holding the real power behind his throne—had been against them. To be sure Gallicans were quite used to playing such games as this with Rome in order to explain away Papal prohibitions, and, since the Sorbonne had refused to 'receive' or 'publish' the Bull (it was only inscribed in the registers), the Assemblée du clergé had refused to accept it at all, and the Paris Parlement had been opposed to it, perhaps for a time it seemed like just another round in tug-of-war between the Gallicans and the Ultra-Montanes.

In the year 1646 the Syndic of the Sorbonne was Nicolas Cornet, a man known for his hostility towards the Jansenists. Cornet had been educated by the Jesuits, had actually entered his noviciate with them and, as related by an editor of Arnauld's *Œuvres complètes*, had been barred only by ill-health from becoming a Jesuit in his own right. It was on the initiative of Cornet that the Sorbonne, early in the year 1646, condemned as heresy part of the 'Preface' composed by Saint-Cyran's nephew, Barcos, that had been attached to Arnauld's famous treatise on communion. The author was called to account for stating that the 'Church had two spiritual heads, St Peter and St Paul, and that [together] these heads formed a single one.' In Rome's view, it was dangerous to state, even metaphorically, that the Church had *two* spiritual heads, because the Pope, St Peter's descendant, was *one*, not two. By implication, the author seemed to be making way for those who, in the Gallican Church, considered themselves disciples of St Paul; in fact he might be trying to raise them to parity with the Pope.

The Holy Office issued a decree condemning the 'Proposition des deux chefs' shortly after the condemnation by the Sorbonne, and thus for the first time since Richelieu, the Faculty of Theology of the University of Paris stood with Rome in the condemnation of a Jansenist. The Parlement of Paris, on the other hand, maintained its usual posture of hostility towards Rome: all copies of the decree of the Holy Office were seized by its order as soon as they reached Paris.

In July 1646 Cornet made a second attempt in the Sorbonne, bringing before the Faculty a series of propositions, five of which were thought to derive from the *Augustinus* of Jansenius.[1] He could trust in their condemnation if only because of the numerous votes in the Sorbonne's 'monks', who would side with Rome and the Jesuits. In fact the mendicants often used the procedure referred to as 'opiner du bonnet'—simply voting as their leaders did, without presuming to examine the issues for themselves. Over the vehement protest of certain members of the secular clergy in the Sorbonne, a commission was immediately constituted to deliberate on the five propositions. As a last effort to head off what seemed like an inevitable condemnation, seventy Doctors of Theology, Arnauld among them, appealed directly to Parlement, protesting the illegality of a commission that had only been established because so many mendicants had voted. Parlement responded favourably and, late in August 1649, it forbade publication of any censure drawn up by the commission; it also forbade all discussion of Cornet's articles as well as the publication of anything treating the issue.

There the matter rested, rather uneasily, while Paris concerned itself with the events of La Fronde. But the tide was running out

---

[1] I Quelques commandements de Dieu sont impossibles aux hommes justes, lors même qu'ils veulent et s'efforcent de les accomplir, selon les forces qu'ils ont présentes; et la grâce leur manque, par laquelle ils leur soient rendus possibles.

II Dans l'état de nature corrompue on ne résiste jamais à la grâce intérieure.

III Pour mériter et démériter dans l'état de nature corrompue, la liberté qui exclut la nécessité n'est pas requise en l'homme, mais suffit la liberté qui exclut la contrainte.

IV Les semi-Pélagiens admettaient la nécessité de la grâce intérieure prévenante pour chaque acte en particulier, même pour le commencement de la foi, et ils étaient hérétiques en ce qu'ils voulaient que cette grâce fût telle que la volonté humaine pût lui résister ou lui obéir.

V C'est semi-Pélagianisme de dire que Jésus-Christ est mort ou qu'il a répandu son sang généralement pour tous les hommes.

for the Jansenists. Mazarin was being informed by their enemies (quite falsely, it would seem) that they were conspiring against him with Paul de Gondi, the future Cardinal de Retz. Although the Nuncio was momentarily blocked in the Sorbonne, he arranged a direct appeal to all the bishops, and, in the spring of 1651, he sent the Pope the letter mentioned earlier which was signed by some sixty French bishops, requesting an official Papal examination of the five points. Later there were said to be over eighty signatures.

The machinery was now set into motion that would lead to disaster for Arnauld in the Sorbonne, as well as to the writing of the first *Provinciales*: The Pope, Innocent X, glad to oblige the French bishops, set up a commission to examine the five points, which would deliberate for two years. Both the Jansenists and their adversaries sent delegations to the Vatican to plead their causes. The Pope himself attended many meetings of the examining commission, and he granted audiences to each delegation, treating the Jansenists with such cordiality indeed that they found it difficult to reconcile this behaviour with the harsh fact that, less than two weeks after their audience with him, the Pope promulgated the famous Bull, *Cum Occasione*, which condemned all the five points as heresy (31 May 1653).' The King of France was informed officially of the condemnation, as were the bishops, in briefs that arrived in Paris one month later. On the advice of his Council, the King by-passed the usual procedure of 'registration' by Parlement and immediately delivered Letters patent to the bishops ordering publication of the Bull in all dioceses and declaring that neither he nor his Council had found anything therein contrary to the liberties of the Gallican Church or to the privileges of the realm.

Chancellor Séguier took charge of drawing up the King's letters, and Mazarin convoked the bishops currently in Paris to meetings in the Louvre. He himself presided over the deliber-

---

[1]Influential in eliciting this Bull was the Compagnie du Saint-Sacrement, a secret society that worked most effectively against the Jansenists. See George Collas, 'Les Provinciales dans la polémique de leur temps', *Les Amis de St François*, No. 80 (1959), p. 26 ff.

tions to see that the prelates subscribed to the King's and the Pope's wishes, which they did by signing a letter to the Pope promising that the Bull would be adhered to in their dioceses. Consequently, the Bull condemning the five points was accepted throughout France.

Certainly the Jansenists were not happy about the condemnation of the five points, and one might wonder how they managed to put up with the decision. The key to their behaviour was the conviction of many Jansenists that the five points were not actually to be found in the *Augustinus*: in fact, they declared, Jansenius had never stated the doctrines attributed to him by Cornet. Arnauld was able to provide textual quotations from the *Augustinus* proving that Jansenius had believed the exact opposite of all but one of the five points, and he declared himself ready to disavow the points wherever they might be found. On the other hand (and how the Jansenists were able to reconcile these two points of view is an interesting problem of casuistry), certain other Jansenists, such as the delegates in Rome—and even Arnauld himself on occasion—maintained that the five points, if correctly interpreted, were quite orthodox and represented the true doctrine of Jansenius and St Augustine. The difficulty was that they had been phrased ambiguously and, if taken in another sense, might imply Calvinist heresy. In accepting the Papal condemnation of the five points, the Jansenists could argue that the Pope had not intended to attack St Augustine and his disciples, but only the false interpretation.

Despite these explanations, the situation was uneasy. The Jansenists must have hoped ardently that there would be no further discussion of the question. But of course the Jesuits were not content to leave the Jansenists with such a large loophole. Father Annat, S.J., who was shortly to become confessor to Louis XIV, protested that the five points were taken directly from Jansenius, 'in so many words' (*totidem verbis*)—a phrase he may secretly have lived to regret, since the evidence to the contrary was clear. Mazarin also seems to have had his own somewhat cynical reasons for not letting the matter stay where it was. Again he summoned the bishops in Paris to a special meeting on the Louvre. Under the prodding of the anti-Jansenist faction they declared firstly that (contrary to the position taken by Arnauld) the five points were the authentic doctrine of Jansenius and, secondly, that (contrary to the view of the Jansenist delegates in Rome) the Papal Bull had condemned these doctrines in their natural and proper sense—in the sense in which Jansenius himself had intended them to be understood. It was also mentioned that the aid of the secular arm might be invoked against any who were recalcitrant. All the bishops signed a letter to the Pope to this effect, even the bishops—and the Archbishop of Sens—who, sympathising with the Jansenists, had protested most forcefully against such a declaration.

One might think this capitulation would have satisfied the enemies of Jansenism. But this was not so. In May 1655, Mazarin convoked for a third time an extraordinary meeting of the bishops currently in Paris. This time the prelates agreed that the Bull and the declarations concerning the five points must not only be accepted but *subscribed to* in every diocese in France. The decisions of the three extraordinary meetings of prelates would not have their full effect until confirmed by the regular meeting of the Assemblée du clergé; but it was clear that episcopal support for the Jansenists had almost totally collapsed. Soon there would not be enough air left for the Jansenists to breathe.

Not that the Jansenists showed any signs of giving up: when their great friend, le Duc de la Rochefoucault-Liancourt was refused absolution by his confessor on account of his Jansenist sympathies, Arnauld, in February and in July, 1655, produced two of his finest defences of Jansenism, *Lettre à une personne de condition . . .* , *Seconde lettre à un duc et pair de France . . .* On the other hand, their enemies were watchful: nine refutations of the first *Lettre* appeared within the space of just a few days after its publication. Complaints about the *Seconde Lettre* furnished the new Syndic of the Sorbonne with the pretext he needed to bring Arnauld's doctrine for judgment before the faculty, on 4 November 1655. Thanks again in part to the votes of the mendicants, an examining commission of six members was instituted to consider Arnauld's *Seconde Lettre*. Among those chosen to sit on the commission were Nicolas Cornet, who had originally proposed the five points to the Faculty of Theology, Alphonse Lemoine, who had given a course of public lectures in the Sorbonne refuting Jansenist doctrines, and Father Nicolaï, a Dominican who turned out to be susceptible to pressure from the Jesuits. After due deliberation the commission made its report, which charged Arnauld with 'temerity' on two counts: (1) his suggestion that the five points might not be found in the *Augustinus*, contrary to the opinion of Rome and the bishops assembled by Mazarin, and (2) a declaration that seemed to support the first of the five points recently condemned by the Papal Bull: '. . . les Pères . . . nous montrent, en la personne de St Pierre, un juste à qui la grâce, sans laquelle on ne peut rien, a manqué dans une occasion où l'on ne peut pas dire qu'il n'ait pas péché . . .' Following the legalistic terminology used in such matters, the first statement was called a *question de fait*, because the question of whether or not the five points actually were in the *Augustinus* was thought to be essentially factual, rather than interpretive. The second statement, on the other hand, was called a *question de droit*, because the problem of St Peter's lapse involved interpretation of an article of doctrine.

The ensuing debates on Arnauld in the Sorbonne were long and frequently tumultuous. Learning he would be allowed no freedom of debate, Arnauld chose not to appear in person, but to have his statement of defence read for him in the Sorbonne, and it was in the sessions after this reading that the tumult reached its height. Time and again the speakers defending Arnauld found it impossible to make themselves heard above the uproar. The historian of the University of Paris relates that at one of the meetings Monsieur de Péréfixe, later Archbishop of Paris, became so exasperated he decided to leave the hall instantly. Rushing towards the door he dragged and knocked down the Bishop of Chartres, while one of the onlookers taunted him with the words of the Apostle, that it is not permitted for a bishop to become angry: *Non vult Apostolus episcopum esse iracundum*. A few steps away, the Dean of the Company, Maître Messier, called over to some partisans of Arnauld, threatening them with the Bastille. They replied sarcastically that, after such menaces, all that remained was to summon the executioner.

It was under pretext of restoring order that the Chancellor of France, Pierre Séguier, suddenly appeared in the Sorbonne, officially uninvited and unannounced, placing himself on the right hand of the Dean (20 December 1655). Since he declared he was acting on orders of the King, no one dared oppose his presiding at the meetings, yet the Jansenists felt this to be a great blow to the freedom of the debate, since everyone was aware of the Chancellor's partisanship. Arnauld made one final effort to head off the vote, by sending a new declaration of submission to the Dean of the Faculty. The document is not without poignancy:

> Quoique j'aie toujours respecté l'autorité et les droits des évêques, et que je sois encore prêt à donner ma vie pour les defendre, il est arrivé, contre mon intention et à ma grande douleur, que plusieurs personnes, entre celles que je respecte le plus, ont été choquées de certains passages d'une lettre que j'ai été obligé récemment d'écrire pour ma defense, par lesquels je mets en doute si les cinq propositions se trouvent dans Jansenius. Si j'avois pensé que ces passages seroient pris en mauvais part, je proteste que je me serois gardé de les écrire, et que je voudrois aujourd'hui ne les avoir jamais écrits. Je demande humblement pardon au pape et aux évêques de les avoir écrits.

The adversaries remained unmoved. The deliberations went on, and, on 14 January 1656, the votes being counted on the *question de fait*, Arnauld was condemned for his temerity in suggesting that the five points were not in Jansenius. The score was 124 votes for condemning Arnauld to 73 votes against the condemnation, plus a number of neutral votes and abstentions.

There remained the vote on the *question de droit*, and, because the debates threatened to be very long, it was ruled that each speaker would be allowed just one half-hour by the hour-glass—referred to as '*le sable*'. Again the Jansenists felt that this measure was unfair because, in view of the previous vote, the only chance left to them was to persuade the Company by discourse. To be sure, in their hearts they must have known that Arnauld was doomed in the Sorbonne.

Tradition has it that at this juncture, when everything seemed hopeless, Arnauld called upon a brilliant young convert to the cause, Blaise Pascal, saying, 'Vous qui êtes jeune, vous devriez faire pour quelque chose' [sic]. The first *Provinciale* appeared while the debates on the *question de droit* were entering the final stage, and the second was completed just as the news of his condemnation was being learned. But by then Arnauld's sympathizers, despairing of obtaining justice in a court where everything was arranged to favour their opponents, had decided to boycott the meetings.

Chapter II

The 'Provincial Letters' as Literature and Theology

Letters I—II

Pascale's *Provinciales* with their graceful style and their fine irony took the debate away from the Latin-speaking world of the clerics, and even from the sober-minded laymen for whom Arnauld had written. Applying the Jansenist practice of vulgarization in a daringly new way, the 'Provincial Letters' brought the whole quarrel into the *salon*, and appealed to the well-bred persons Pascal found there to play the role of judges of theology.

In thus seeking a new audience Pascal becomes, in a very real sense, a precursor of Montesquieu and Voltaire who would imitate this same tactic in their campaign against Catholic superstition and intolerance. Indeed one of the implications of the word 'philosophe' in the eighteenth century was, as Professor Dieckmann has pointed out,[1] that the author would be addressing precisely the kind of well-bred person for whom Pascal was writing and that, like Pascal, he would charm not only the gentlemen, but even the ladies, making them arrive effortlessly at desirable conclusions concerning difficult subjects. Occasionally with the 'philosophes' this tactic slips into a kind of mannerism: they are putting on a performance to entertain the company and we are aware that they have deliberately gilded the pill. The miracle of Pascal is, of course, the feeling he gives us of utter freshness and spontaneity, carrying the reader along so rapidly he doesn't

[1] *Le Philosophe; texts and interpretation* (Saint Louis, Missouri, 1948).

have time to detect the contrivances employed. To be sure, Pascal's procedure of bringing the debate into the drawing-room was not without its inconveniences, even in the seventeenth-century context; for the mundane persons he was addressing were clearly *not* competent judges of theology; there was no possibility of presenting the issues in their full dimension—they would first have to be won over by the entertainment. The first two Letters are especially striking in this regard: the reader is assured at the outset that no deep understanding of theology will be required of him—in fact he is informed that the only real issues in the vote against Arnauld had been political, not theological; hence the problem of finding out whether the five points really were in the *Augustinus*—the *question de fait*—becomes almost irrelevant. As for the *question de droit*, the issues are actually so simple, in fact, so trivial, that one can become an expert in no time at all—as the reader will soon see.

As if by a miracle Pascal turns the technicalities of 'proximate power' and 'sufficient grace' into the most sparkling, witty dialogues in which spokesmen for the various points of view—Jesuit, Thomist or Jansenist—attempt to initiate the bewildered narrator into the mysteries of the debate. Incredibly, religious controversy becomes a *divertissement*, whose humour is not at all the forced Sunday-school brand so familiar in Calvinist countries, but genuine comedy, an endless reservoir of laughter, the kind of abundant source that Molière tapped when creating *Les Fâcheux*. The narrator's innocent bewilderment is only a trap, of course, his apparent guilelessness serving to entice the opponents out into the open and then to reveal for all the world to see how absurd the terms of the debate really are. As the dislogues proceed and the Jesuits and Thomists more and more fall prey to the narrator's concealed irony, their positions on 'sufficient grace' seem to be withering away, threatening finally to shrivel into a playful clatter of nonsense syllables.

In the twentieth century we inevitably miss part of the fun of these Letters because we no longer have any expectations concerning the style in which theological subjects should be treated. But in Pascal's time sufficient grace and proximate power called for an elevated language, and preferably one that would keep these delicate topics from the eyes of persons unfit to see them, such as common people, and, more generally, women. Pascal was bitterly reproached by the Jesuits for not using Latin. They were offended, too, that instead of employing the rolling cadences of the *style noble*, he descended the scale all the way down to one of the lowest styles, the satirical dialogue. To the Jesuits and their allies it was clear that the author was making a mockery of theological disputations.

Perhaps Pascal's own newness to these particular controversies helped him set the tone so perfectly here; the feigned innocence of the narrator, the round-eyed surprise he displays as the true nature of the dispute unwinds itself before him, reflects, perhaps, the real innocence of Pascal, not too long before. The impudence is the impudence of the relatively young man he was. Above all, Pascal's acute sense of the absurdity of the quarrel suggests a certain freshness of approach: longer familiarity with the terms of the controversy might have diminished their capacity to provoke mirth.

The situation Pascal describes might seem to call for some high-handed irony: the Sorbonne, in considering the *question de fait*, did not condemn Arnauld for *error* in doubting that the five points were in Jansenius, but for *temerity* in contradicting the Pope who, both implicitly in a Constitution and explicitly in a brief, had said they were, and whose condemnation had been approved by the French bishops. Not truth, but simple obedience to ecclesiastical authority had been declared the only issue and, though they tried again and again, the Jansenists were blocked from bringing to the floor the question of whether, or not, the five points actually were in the *Augustinus* as the Pope and the Assemblée du clergé had stated. Here is the Duc de Luynes' account of one of the deliberations (18 December, 1655):

M. de Mincé a renouvellé la requisition faitte dès hier pour examiner si les V. Propositions sont dans Jansenius, & M.

Brousse qui opinoit le premier aujourd'hui l'aiant appuyée &
continuant à parler trop longtemps au gré des Evêques sur ce
sujet ils se sont mis à l'interrompre & à le menacer du Roy
[...] Ils se sont emportez jusqu'à parler de prisons & de
chastimens, & que le Chancelier viendroit dans l'Assemblée,
ce qui a fort irrité les esprits: de sorte que tout le reste du temps
s'est consumé en tumultes. Les Evêques se sont levez en continuant leurs menaces & particulierement M. de Rodez [...]
Enfin l'on ne peut rien ajoûter à ces violences[...][B. N., Fonds
français, 13896, fol. 6, verso (copy).]

Since the Sorbonne had so firmly, even violently, excluded
from discussion the alleged Jansenist origins of the five points, it
was perhaps appropriate that Pascal also should brush aside this
matter in the opening *Provinciales*, and not even pretend to
examine the substance of the question. In any case, it is clear that
the superficiality of Pascal's presentation here is deliberate,[1] and
not, as has often been suggested, due to mere ignorance or lack of
theological training. Pascal's earlier interests may have been
slightly more scientific than theological, but the Jansenists had
developed a strong tradition of vulgarization, and had Pascal
only studied Arnauld's two recently published *Lettres*, he would
have come a long way towards understanding the theology he
discusses here. We also know that while composing the *Provinciales*, he was in constant touch with theologians such as Arnauld
and Nicole, who furnished him with many of the references he
used, and would certainly have given him explanations of
doctrine, had he needed them. Even if Madame Périer's story
that her twelve-year-old brother had re-invented thirty-two
propositions of Euclid for himself unaided is something of an
exaggeration, Pascal's geometrical treatise on conic sections, his
arithmetical calculating machine (dedicated to Chancellor
Séguier), and the repetition of Toricelli's experiments on atmos-
pheric pressure already had born witness to his genius in science,
and the *Provinciales*, masterful distortions that they are, suggest

---

[1]See Philippe Sellier, *Pascal et St. Augustin* (Paris: Colin, 1970).

an exceptionally able theologian as well as a comic genius.

The first two *Provinciales* concentrate particularly upon the Thomists, and in this orientation they directly reflect the debates then in progress in the Sorbonne. Doctrinally the Thomists stood at the exact mid-point between the Jansenists and the Jesuits: with the former they held that efficacious grace was absolutely necessary for salvation. Yet they were not willing to state with the Jansenists that God gave men commandments they were unable to obey, or that men were condemned for sins of which they were not aware. Instead, using terms similar to those of the Jesuits, they stated that God also gave men 'sufficient' grace, enabling them, theoretically, to overcome temptation and to practice virtue. They also conceded, contrary to the Jesuits, that 'sufficient' grace never actually became efficacious; in fact, it was never 'sufficient' in the literal sense of the term. The only polemical advantage of Thomistic theology seems to be that it avoided the impious dilemma attributed to the Jansenists: that God, having made certain man had no wings, then ordered him to fly.

Both before and during the debates in the Sorbonne there were attempts to use Thomism as a compromise by which to settle the controversy out of court: if only the Jansenists would subscribe to the Thomistic formula (which actually originated with St Thomas's modern disciples), many bishops, and Mazarin also, hoped that peace might be obtained. Yet, almost predictably, Arnauld had proved intransigent: he would admit nothing that diluted the power of efficacious grace. Consequently, in the Sorbonne, willingness or unwillingness to recognize 'sufficient' grace had become a sort of touchstone in the debates, a rallying point for the opponents of Jansenism. Cornet declared in his address that Arnauld's refusal to subscribe to sufficient grace was what rendered him and his doctrine inexcusable.

Pascal, in turn, adopts a hard line in the first two *Provinciales*, showing with pitiless clarity, and with a masterfully comic touch, the ridiculousness, even the bad faith, of those who would call 'sufficient' something that, by their own admission, *never* sufficed, and 'proximate' a power that was never literally proximate. Surely the Thomists must see the point: to admit this ambiguous wording which, precisely because of its ambiguity had been subscribed to by the Jesuits, represented a capitulation to the Jesuit version of sufficient grace and proximate power. Because the issue seemed so momentous, Pascal added an appeal to the Thomists, urging them not to abandon the great tradition of efficacious grace as it had been handed down in sacred trust from St Augustine, St Bernard, and from St Thomas himself. In Pascal's mind there was no question but that the Thomists really belonged in the Jansenists' camp.

Perhaps tactically, Pascal may have gone a little too far in his mocking caricature: Father Nicolaï, the Thomist referred to in the *Provinciales*—who was also a member of the Commission judging Arnauld's doctrines—indignantly rejected the idea that there was an implicit doctrinal entente between the Jansenists and the Thomists. Fearing that Pascal's Letters had needlessly offended potential allies, Pierre Nicole, in his Latin translation of the *Provinciales*, did his best in a note to show that Pascal had not really intended to satirize Thomistic doctrines; for some of the Jansenists, it became standard practice to say they agreed with sufficient grace in the Thomistic sense; one Jansenist author had quoted a passage from the *Augustinus* in which Jansenius expressed a rather ironic attitude towards the Thomistic position; however, once the passage was lifted from its original context, it just might pass for a straight forward eulogy . . .

Today, we are less concerned about Thomistic difficulties over sufficient grace and we are freer than Father Nicolaï was to enjoy Pascal's narrator as he rushes from one theologian to another, struggling and straining to attach just some meaning to their mystifying pronouncements: thinking he has caught on, but finding he is further in the dark than ever, and then stumbling at last into the daylight—only to discover that the object of his elaborate chase had been a very silly-looking rabbit indeed: an absurdity, an inconsistency, people not saying the words they mean.

There is such gaiety and fun in these first two Letters, we marvel that they could ever have come from gloomy Jansenism at such a gloomy time. The key here is the point sometimes brought out by modern critics, that comedy—and most especially satire—may actually reflect considerable hatred and anger, whose cutting edge has been converted into laughter. Traditionally, religious polemicists liked to see themselves, in metaphor, as gladiators in the arena, and in the dialogues of the *Provinciales* also, one sometimes has the impression that, metaphorically, Pascal is cornering an adversary and slaying his argument. Yet, at the same time, if one wanted to describe Pascal's procedure in metaphor, one would choose terms that come less from battles and combats than from such things—and this is often true in satire—as pillories, whipping-posts and scapegoats.

Letters III—IV

Just before the appearance of the third *Provinciale* the vote on the *question de droit* had been taken and not only had Arnauld's doctrine been censured, but he himself had been formally excluded from the Sorbonne. For the Faculty of Theology to act thus towards one of its members was a most unusual occurrence, in fact there was very little recent precedent for it. The Faculty also decreed that every student must swear an oath disavowing Arnauld's doctrines, and here again the measure was unusual. Since Arnauld's sympathizers had decided to boycott the meetings, the vote against him had been numerically overwhelming. Nor should one underestimate the importance of the doctrine condemned: as their opponents reminded them time and again in the debates, the Jansenist interpretation of St Peter's lapses set clearly in relief their concept of an inscrutable deity justly inflicting punishments on wicked humanity for sins men could not have avoided, and of which they were not even aware. Although Arnauld's condemnation was engineered largely by persons outside the Sorbonne, it represented a significant trend within the Faculty of Theology also: it had now become clear that, thanks to the votes of the 'monks' and to the forceful eloquence of such persons as the current Archbishop of Toulouse, who was as hostile to Arnauld and his partisans as the old one had been favourable, the alliance of the Gallicans in the Sorbonne and the Jansenists was no longer adequate to save them.

Nevertheless, in just the opening pages of the third *Provinciale*, Pascal, with the most deft sleight of hand, manages to turn this mountainous condemnation and rejection of the Jansenists into the merest mouse at which all could laugh in scorn and relief: now it is for the Sorbonne to explain how in the world it could have produced such a miserable object as this. The trick he uses, in addition to the marvels of his prose style—the clarity, the force, the economy, the wit, and just a hint of the fullness of the emotions he felt in this time of distress—is to ignore the complicated *question de droit* concerning St Peter's lapse and treat it instead as if it were simply a *question de fait*: Is it true that St Augustine and other Fathers of the Church had written phrases similar to those composed by Arnauld? He handily proves that they had, and concludes that, since Arnauld was only repeating what St Augustine had declared before him, his condemnation must be attributed to pure malevolence against the leader of the Jansenists. The rest is so easy, the letter almost naturally evolves into comedy.

Pierre Nicole hinted in his Latin translation of the Provincial Letters that although this work seemed superficially to be as spontaneous and disorganized as real letters often are, it might actually have some sort of unified structure. Since Nicole was one of those who furnished Pascal with arguments and references for his Provincial Letters, he may also have had a hand in determining their shape, and one would do well to ponder his suggestion. Our own age has rejected so much that was handed down to it: it may seem a fearfully long way back from the fragmentation and isolation characterizing our own contemporary perspective to the cosmic Christian view of Pascal's time, but the unity of the 'Provincial Letters' certainly derives from this. Perhaps we would already have been aware of it had not Pascal deliberately suppressed the links binding his topics together.

Letter I deals with *le pouvoir prochain*, Letter II with *la grâce suffisante*, and no mention is ever made of the connection between them; in fact they are treated as though they belonged to two entirely separate, and equally comical, species. But of course they are in reality very closely connected one with another: 'proximate power' is a power of sufficient grace, so that to some extent the terms actually represent the same theological phenomenon viewed in two different perspectives, although sufficient grace is a more inclusive conception. Letter III, with its telling Scriptural example of St Peter's lapses, actually concerns the Jansenist alternative to sufficient grace: efficacious grace. Letter IV seems again to be raising a new issue: the contention of the Jesuits that for a sin to be counted against a man, he must realize he is offending God and deliberately sin nevertheless, a concept which Pascal easily shows to be absurd. What he does not tell us is that this Jesuit doctrine is another manifestation of their sufficient grace. In sum, the first four Letters concern sufficient versus efficacious grace, although to the uninitiated they might seem like a grab-bag of comical Jesuit fallacies.

Pascal's breaking up of Jesuit doctrine into those small bits whose absurdity springs out as self-evident is certainly an effective technique: it reduces the pieces of information the reader must swallow to sizes that neither choke nor produce a depressing feeling of over-indulgence. The massive, viscous coherence of Jesuit theology is far from being a laughing matter, yet these light, brittle pieces, handled so skilfully by Pascal, are ideally suited to comedy. Finally, the fragmentation and isolation of the parts of doctrine in a context of absurdity, is what makes Pascal seem so astonishingly close to our modern age, fragmented and absurd as so much of our experience has come to seem,[1] while the noble coherence of both the Jesuit and the Jansenist theological systems remains, for most of us, somehow out of reach.

---

[1] A somewhat different approach to this topic will be found in Carlo François, *La Notion de l'absurde dans la litétrature française du XVIIe siècle* (Paris, 1973), pp. 96—100.

Letters V—X

In Pascal's age a curious sense of *hierarchy* seems to have pervaded everything, not only in life, but in the arts as well: in music, the trumpets and drums were sometimes placed at the top of the score, no matter how seldom these instruments were sounded, just as in the librettos of tragedy the parts of kings and queens were traditionally listed before all others, whether or not these personages had many lines to speak. In painting, either religious scenes or 'tableaux d'histoire' recording the crownings of monarchs, the births of princes and battles royal took pride of place over all other genres, even though the real artistic talents of the century may have lain in something quite different, such as landscapes, or smiling cupids or 'portraits de caractère'. In religion, theology *always* preceded ethics, although the two were closely bound together, and although there already existed in Pascal's time a tendency to stress ethics which eventually would come to undermine theology. Nevertheless, in the seventeenth century, the first questions one raised invariably concerned such matters as the Trinity, or predestination and the workings of grace; morality came second. The reason for this order was certainly the ancient tradition that it is more fitting to consider the nature of God and His laws before one turns to the conduct of man. At the same time the arrangement was logical because it assumed that a virtuous life grew out of one's Christian beliefs: if one knew God and loved Him as one should, this would inform all the actions of one's life.

This sense of order perhaps explains the horror Pascal expressed in Letter V as he contemplated the Jesuits' practice of putting ethical expedience first and then tailoring theology to fit in with their morals, corrupt though they might be. Not only was this practice damaging to certain articles of faith, it represented for Pascal a kind of perversion, a twisting of the natural order of things. Perhaps it is appropriate that the character of the Jesuit in these Letters—bland, soft, patient, never angry except when forced to look straight at the corrupt consequences of his doctrines, an eager displayer of illicit wares—has something of the pimp or of the go-between abuot it. The role of the narrator, on the other hand, is ambiguous for different reasons. On those rather rare occasions when he reveals his true feelings he provides an exact counterpoise to the Jesuit: hot-tempered, indignant, uncompromising, very much committed to the defence of Christian ethics. Yet much of the time the narrator chooses rather to hide his real emotions under a mask that deceptively leads the Jesuit to think that he and the Reverend Fathers are being applauded in their feats of casuistry, so that he will unsuspectingly reveal the whole depth of his immorality. Paradoxically we find here a kind of innocence on the part of the Jesuit as he runs breathlessly from folio to folio, proudly putting his finger on the marvels of a casuistry which finds explanations and excuses for almost anything, whereas the narrator, urging him on, exclaiming in astonishment over the doctrines he reads, pretending his only fear is that the casuistry will prove unable to render innocuous such things as lying, murder and adultery, is not without duplicity. Of course, Pascal is only beating the Jesuits at their own game, since it was the Jesuit casuists who had claimed that it was permitted to say one thing out loud, while secretly under one's breath meaning another. Moreover, the narrator's role, all interest and enthusiasm for the Jesuit, while winking at the reader and playfully inviting him to join in the conspiracy to see just how far the Jesuit will go, makes an effect that is perhaps more theatrical than literary: Pascal is staging an entertainment, and like the 'straight man' in a comedy, the narrator's playing along with the Jesuit makes the satire doubly vivid, while, at the same time, his own feigned indifference to the evil of the Jesuit's doctrine becomes an irresistible invitation for the spectator to condemn it for himself.

In all of these devices Pascal seems closer to the eighteenth century than he does to the early part of the reign of Louis XIV: the feigned innocence of Montesquieu's Persians seems just two steps away, and, seen against a background of Jansenist austerity, all the elaborate constructions of Pascal's Jesuit, citing casuists who wriggle and squirm their miserable way out of tight corners, and which the Jesuit presents replete with references to pages and editions, as if he were showing off some marvel of the age, pave the way for Voltaire's narrator in the *Lettres philoso-phiques*—bowing, scraping, plumes a-flutter, all oaths and compliments, coming before the grave, upright Quaker who does not even care to remove his hat.

From a literary standpoint, the comedy of the Letters on Casuistry is probably Pascal's most brilliant achievement. In fact, so masterful is the presentation, and so convincing the argument, that to this day the Society of Jesus has never fully recovered; for multitudes of French persons the word 'Jesuit' instantly conjures up, before all else, the unforgettable figure of the casuist created here by Pascal.

Transformations of Source Material

One of the notable features of these Letters on Casuistry is the feeling Pascal gives us that the material itself—the actual quotations from the casuists—is doing all the work for him. Pascal has merely to give the bough a gentle shake and the fruit will drop of its own weight. If we laugh, or become indignant, it is simply because the Jesuits themselves are behaving laughably, or infamously, and never—and here Pascal's strategy differs significantly from that of someone like Voltaire—because the author is being so clever. By the same token, the role of the narrator, so innocently curious and so modestly ignorant, functions as a kind of blank slate that continually invites the Jesuit himself to spell out the letter of his doctrines; and if, time and again, the Jesuit finds himself trapped, the fault is always what he himself has been saying, and never—or so it seems—the narrator's artful contrivances.

On the other hand, the moment one sets Pascal's brilliant pages beside the lumbering denunciations from the pens of his Jansenist colleagues, one sees why Nicole spoke of the Letters on Casuistry in awesome tones as Pascal's most significant accomplishment.

We discover that, contrary to the impression Pascal gives us, he has totally transformed his material while recreating it as comedy. There is nothing inherently funny about Jesuit casuistry at all, though Pascal has charmed us into thinking there was; indeed, in its natural state, seventeenth-century casuistry numbers among history's most tiresome topics.

One of Pascal's priceless quotations, presented with a marvellously light touch in the middle of the ninth *Provinciale*, comes from Father Garasse, S.J., who actually argued against condemning self-satisfaction as a sin because, he declared, God would have wanted the frogs to feel satisfied with themselves at the conclusion of their songs'.

Now, Father Garasse does have a certain importance in the intellectual history of seventeenth-century France, if only because he was an early opponent of St Cyran, and because he wrote so much against those he called 'atheists' and 'libertines'. On the other hand, it is difficult to assess the merits of a number of his works because of a certain deranged quality that informs much of them—one often wonders if he really knows what he is saying. Above all, one should not try to read him for mirth: his angry accusations, the endless rantings, and the hopeless confusion of many of his arguments, make for painful reading today. It is only Pascal's genius that allows us to have, through Father Garasse, a delightful moment of comedy.

One might make a similar observation concerning the passages quoted by Pascal (Letter V, near the beginning) from the *Imago primi Sæculi*, the beautifully printed, handsomely illustrated *Festschrift* the Jesuits wrote for themselves to celebrate their hundredth birthday. Having been trained by Pascal to see the Jesuits as unprincipled, ambitious condoners of corruption, it comes as a drole surprise to find them, in the quotations given by Pascal, comparing themselves, not to men, but to that troop of light, speedy angels predicted in Isaiah ('Allez, anges prompts et légers'), calling themselves 'eagle spirits', 'phoenixes', and saying they have, since their birth, changed the face of Christendom.

¹Provinciales, ed. Louis Cognet (Paris = Garnier, 1965), p. 161.

'Il faut le croire, puisqu'ils le disent', comments Pascal's narrator, neatly pricking their balloon. He then goes on to discuss in an entirely serious way the principles of behaviour of the Society of Jesus, giving a picture of the Jesuits, incidentally, that, while far from flattering, is distinctly fairer than the one given later, in Letter IX, where Pascal tries to make even the moderate Jesuits somehow responsible for the excesses of the immoderates.

But of course the phrases from the *Imago* about the angels, eagle spirits and phoenixes, undermined by the strong irony of the context in which they appear, actually become caricatures, ridiculous lampoons, that in their utter absurdity turn against the persons they had been designed to support and even to adorn. And yet the work from which these metaphors come could hardly be less entertaining. As its title might suggest, the *Imago* is an endless exercise in narcissism: sickeningly unctuous, fatuous in tone, only Pascal's genius could have turned any part of it into an object of our delight.[1]

But then, so many qualities in Pascal's comedy of casuistry are unique with him: the perfect mixture of the serious and the comic—each serving to set off the other, the constant variety in the tone, the liveliness of a dialogue composed, unbelievably, of actual quotations from grave casuists, the intuitive sense of just how long to stay on any one topic, the suspense that builds from Letter to Letter, all these things set the *Provinciales* in another world from the edifying treatises of his Jansenist friends who plow their way so systematically through all the points, major and minor.

The Structure of the Letters on Casuistry

Judging by internal evidence, it is clear that, from the start, the Letters on Casuistry had been planned as a series (doubtless with Nicole's help), and that enormous care was taken in organizing them—indeed this effort to plan the whole may have been one of the causes of the delay in the appearance of the Letter V. A

---

[1]For other such transformations see Michel Le Guern, 'Sur la bataille des *Provinciales* . . .', *Revue d'histoire littéraire de la France*, 1966, pp. 293—296. The famous cacophony of names near the end of the fifth *Provinciale* would be another example.

general introduction to the subject of Jesuit casuistry appears in the first letter of the group (Letter V, pp. 74-9), specifying a number of the areas to be covered and even foreshadowing the final culminating Letter on charity (Letter X). Henceforth we are regularly given outlines—usually disguised as dialogue—reviewing points already discussed or telling of those still to come. Thus in the second Letter of the series (Letter VI, p. 104) we find an outline of the contents of three Letters, a plan that is adhered to quite faithfully, and that is later referred to several times. The result of this strategy is economy, of course, and forcefulness, since none of the energy is dissipated in repetitions and overlappings. Above all, thanks to these outlines, we are actually schooled in the subject, learning to see each point the author raises in perspective, as it relates to the whole.

Although the reader may never be conscious of the fact, the structure of these Letters is really quite complex, indeed we may approach some of them from several different viewpoints. First, Letters V-X systematically expose and denounce the four general principles sponsored by the Jesuits that Pascal considered to be the root of all their evil morality: (1) 'Probable opinions', a doctrine enabling them to authorize as 'probable' a multitude of innovations in ethics, no matter how contrary they might be to the ancient traditions of the Church (Letters V and VI); (2) 'Direction of intention', a device by which even such a mortal sin as homicide can be partially 'purified', simply by calling it by a different name: 'the desire to protect one's honour', for example (Letters VII–VIII); (3) The doctrine of 'equivocals' and 'mental restrictions' thanks to which one may deliberately state out loud the opposite of what one knows to be the truth (Letter IX); (4) The sufficiency of 'attrition' in the sacrament of Penance, a doctrine implying that there is no absolute necessity to repent one's sins or even to love God (Letter X). The sacraments and charity become the central issues here.

But while he is denouncing these Jesuit tenets, the sins Pascal uses as illustrations in three of the Letters are carefully grouped according to the social class to which they pertain: sins of the clergy (*bénéficiers, prêtres, religieux*) come first, in Letter VI; then, in Letter VII, we find sins of the nobility (*gentilshommes, leurs domestiques*); finally, in Letter VIII, we have a rather odd group from the Third Estate (judges, usurers, bankrupt persons, thieves, fallen women and sorcerers). The narrator explicitly draws our attention to this arrangement several times (pp. 104, 135, 151); no doubt he wanted us to understand that the evils of Jesuit casuistry afflicted all the classes of society. This was also, of course, the natural way to order things according to the seventeenth-century perspective.

But there is still a third ordering to be observed in some of the Letters on Casuistry, existing simultaneously along with the other two. Some of the sins are also grouped according to more traditional theological lines; in Letter VII, the basic sin throughout is homicide, either out of vengeance or greed. In Letter VIII, it is fraud, involving money or other property. In Letter IX we find a veritable nosegay of vices: ambition, avarice, vanity, envy, sloth, gluttony, lying and adultery, having at least a partial resemblance to the traditional seven deadly sins.

To anyone who has read Dante's *Divine Comedy* this section of the *Provinciales* may almost suggest a parody of a descent into hell: As in Dante, the various sins are paraded before us in careful order, and our guide, like Virgil, explains their nature to us. But, of course, while Virgil's role was to make sure Dante understood the justice of God's punishments by knowing the evil nature of men's vices, our Jesuit guide is there, or so it seems, to make sure God doesn't punish anyone seriously for anything, and to convert all the mortal sins into venial ones. As we descend through the vices of Letter VIII, we even find a sort of inverted order of charity being established in which the Jesuits, on principle, condescend to the weakness and greed of the sinner, at the expense of those he harms. At the bottom of Letter VIII we find, appropriately enough, the Devil being invoked by a sorcerer (p. 148).

The Problem of Pascal's innacuracies

A great deal has been written concerning Pascal's fairness, or unfairness, in his treatment of Jesuit casuistry. The Jesuits themselves led the way in the debate, declaring the 'Secretary of Port Royal' to be fraudulent and dishonest, and of course Pascal devoted five of the *Provinciales* (XII–XVI) to answering their charges. The most serious accusation, and one that has been renewed quite frequently in modern times, was that Pascal had deliberately falsified the quotations he used, changing words, adding or leaving out phrases, and lifting passages from their context, in order to make the casuists seem far worse than they really were.

Now it is undoubtedly true that a certain number of passages have been altered or lifted from context, and that many of these changes strengthen Pascal's hand, however slightly. Indeed it is disconcerting to read in the sixth *Provinciale* that the Jesuit held out a book to the narrator in which the narrator 'saw' certain words that Pascal proceeds to quote—not quite accurately, as one discovers in Abbé Cognet's recent edition (Paris: Garnier, 1965, p. 98). Nor does it seem right to dismiss the matter, as some scholars have tried to do, by arguing that such carelessness was very common in seventeenth-century religious controversies, and that Pascal was no more inaccurate than many others. The truth is that, however careless other controversialists may have been, the Jansenists (like the Protestants) made a point of scrupulous accuracy in their quotations: the number of inaccuracies one finds here in Pascal is quite exceptional in Jansenist literature at this time.

On the other hand, there is no reason to assume that these changes were deliberate on Pascal's part. Though they may have slightly strengthened his argument here and there, in the long run they rather weakened his case since they made him vulnerable to accusations by Jesuits, who, ironically enough, were sometimes far less accurate or honest in their quotations than Pascal had been. But the main point is that Pascal did not need to falsify anything in order to prove his case. The evidence was overwhelmingly in his favour, on all the major issues at least. The Jesuits couldn't refute Pascal's accusations because the vast majority of the passages quoted from the casuists were in fact where Pascal had stated they were, and they lent themselves to the interpretations Pascal said they did. In many instances the Jesuits answering the *Provinciales* didn't even attempt to deny the truth of Pascal's quotations; they merely declared that Pascal was unfair to attribute to Jesuits doctrines that were shared by all manner of casuists—Thomists, or whatever. But this way of arguing proved really quite unconvincing to most because it begged the main question of the charged immorality of Jesuit teachings: the fact that immoral doctrines might be held by many different persons didn't make these doctrines any better. In short, just so long as one accepts Pascal's basic assumptions concerning the nature of sin and the Church's role as arbiter of men's vices (which, of course, our modern, more secular era is quite unprepared to do), his case is really unassailable.

It would seem more reasonable to assume that the inaccuracies crept into Pascal's citations because others had collected most of them for him; only exceptionally, such as with Escobar and, probably, Pirot, did he see the original texts himself. Nor should one forget that the *Provinciales* were published in secret, some of them in haste; there probably was neither time, nor the facilities, to verify the quotations. Other inaccuracies may have crept in as Pascal reworked his material, reshaping it into the astonishing masterpiece we read today. But in any case, the altered quotations didn't change anything essential: When Pierre Nicole later translated the Provincial Letters into Latin, he attempted to correct systematically all the inaccurate quotations and to restore the context of passages when appropriate. The result is a text that is considerably more correct than the French version had been, but at the same time Pascal's attack seems as forceful as ever.

It was suggested earlier that Pascal seems to anticipate certain features of eighteenth-century authors in the satirical devices he uses. The 'Provincial Letters' are also linked to the Enlightenment in the almost conspiratorial air of clandestinity that surrounded them. Of course the mere fact that they appeared anonymously[1] was nothing unusual for the time: it was common practice to publish theological works either under a pseudonym or without any author's name, out of modesty or prudence. But with Pascal anonymity becomes itself a device with which to prick the reader's curiosity, daring him to try to find out who the real author is, taunting him with mysterious clues whose keys are impossible to decipher. Thanks to the safety of being an unknown voice coming from nowhere he did not have to hesitate to challenge the word of the King's confessor, or to deny the infallibility of the Pope in *questions de fait*.

The Jesuits complained angrily of the author's anonymity and tried to turn it to their advantage, saying that since the author was nobody, he was scarcely worth answering. Needless to say their response did not impede the growing popularity of the Letters, which were printed secretly on various presses and, despite police raids and arrests of publishers, continued to be distributed clandestinely in major cities of France.

The success of the *Provinciales* had been quite astonishing; we know this not only from the testimonies of friends of the Jansenists and from the fact that printings and reprintings continued despite real dangers of arrest, but also from the fierce anger they provoked in the opponents. Here is a contemporary account of the discussion in the Sorbonne of the second *Provinciale*:

Hier 10e Feber [1656] apres le Souper en Sorbonne il y eut grande contestation entre des Docteurs Molinistes & des disciples de S. Augustin sur le suiet de la *Seconde Lettre au Provincial*. M. Morel nous dit que c'estoit la methode des heretiques d'escrire ainsi contre les Censures de la Faculte et que Calvin en avoit usé de cette maniere; M. Le Meusnier luy

---

[1]In the first collected edition, Pascal used the pseudonym 'Louis de Montalte', which was immediately recognised to be fictitious. In the *Pensées* (ed. Brunschvicg, No. 52) he suggested that the word 'Provincial' in the title was the invention of the printer, a suggestion that was later con-firmed by Nicole. See Brunschvicg, ed., *Œuvres de Pascal*, XII, p. 56. P. Keuntz, 'Un discours nommé Montalte', *Rev. d'hist. littéraire de la France*, 71 (1971), pp. 195—206, discusses the function of this pseudonym as rhetoric in the *Provinciales*.

dit qu'il y avoit bien de la difference, parce que Calvin
parloit contre les Censures de la Faculte qui avoient determiné
des choses de foy mais que cette lettre ne parloit que de la
maniere dont les choses se passoient. Le dit Sr Morel s'emporta
extraordinairement contre M. Meusnier et M. Queras, leur
dit qu'ils estoient des heretiques qu'ils ne recevoient ny le
Concile de Trente ny la constitution d'Innocent X quoyqu'ils
en firent semblant, qu'ils n'en seroient pas les iuges, mais
l'Eglise et qu'on leur feroit bien voir dans le temps. [B.N.,
Fonds français, 13896, fol. 422 recto.]

In view of open threats such as these, it is not surprising that
the Jansenists would be discreet, sometimes even secretive, in
their movements, that occasionally they would disguise their
communications using special handwriting, and that Pascal
himself would keep very much out of sight while his dangerous
Letters were being printed. A few of his movements have been
traced: sometimes he stayed in nondescript Paris inns, the famous
one being named 'Au Roy David' behind the Sorbonne, where
his brother-in-law, Monsieur Périer, came to join him. A contemporary account relates that on one occasion two Jesuits
came to see him there (one of them being a family relation) and
that they chanced to enter just after he had been brought sheets
of a recent *Provinciale* fresh from the printer—the pages were
still wet. There are several versions of the anecdote and many
differences of detail among them; the most picturesque one
relates that the untimely visit obliged him to put the sheets on
his bed and hide them by pulling the curtains. This version further
states that the relative, on his way out, said to Pascal he should be
warned that people everywhere were saying he was the author
of the 'Provincial Letters', and that he should look to his safety.
Pascal thanked him for the information, adding that he had nothing to fear, that the 'Letters' were attributed to many other
persons with as little justification, and that it was impossible to
prevent people from having suspicions such as these ... (B.N.,
Fonds français, 13895, fol. 280 recto.)

C

Sometimes Pascal stayed in the St Merri Cloister as a guest of the Duc de Roannez; perhaps he also sojourned in the country on the estate of the Duc de Luynes. It is not actually certain whether or not he stayed at the famous 'Granges' at Port-Royal at this time. On the other hand we are sure that, while in hiding, Pascal was constantly being helped by Jansenists more familiar with the controversies than he; indeed virtually all of the erudition of these letters comes from someone else: Arnauld, Nicole, Antoine Lemaitre, and probably others. With the Letters on Jesuit ethics Pascal became increasingly dependent on material which had been collected for him, and this may well have influenced both his subject-matter and his presentation of material. Nor is there any reason to think that such a person as Nicole did not contribute witticisms and entire passages concerning doctrine to Pascal's 'Letters', in addition to references to relevant Jesuit casuists. In this sense the 'Provincial Letters' are the result of a collaboration: Pascal could not have done it alone. Yet it is also true that when it became safer to name the author of the *Provinciales* no knowledgeable Jansenist even thought to attribute this work to anyone but Pascal. Our own age tends to be more finicky about attributions, but in the seventeenth century no one minded when Molière cribbed jokes, lines, passages, situations, scenes and entire plots from comic authors such as Plautus, Terence, Scarron or Cyrano de Bergerac; he, and no one else, was still the author of *Les Fourberies de Scapin*, just as La Fontaine was the author of *La Cigale et la Fourmi* even though it had been adapted almost word for word from the classical text. Arnauld, an admirable writer in many ways, was virtually incapable of wit: there appears to be only one attempt at a real joke in the works certainly attributable to him and, sodden, laboured as it is, sitting alone in a mirthless landscape, the effect is almost grotesque. Nicole was far closer to Pascal both temperamentally and stylistically. Yet even if one chooses the work by Nicole most similar in form and content to the *Provinciales*, one finds something so far below them in verve, wit and imagination, that one is inclined to agree with the seventeenth and eighteenth centuries that the 'Provincial Letters' are the unique masterpiece they are because their author—no matter how much assistance he obtained—was a genius: Pascal.

Letters XI—XVI

The Jesuits were naturally angry to find themselves the butt of so much laughter; they complained that the 'Provincial Letters' made a mockery of holy things. Pascal's reaction to their criticism was a curious one: he first composed the eleventh *Provinciale*, a brilliant defence of the use of humour in behalf of religion. He cites the Bible and the Church Fathers as being in favour of laughing at wickedness. Turning the tables on the opponent, he displays priceless examples of humour—not all of it conscious humour—taken from Jesuits and their friends. Having established the validity of his approach, he then proceeds to abandon comedy entirely for the next five Letters. Instead of staging dialogues personifying the Jesuit and Jansenist, and playing a role that involved a double game himself, Pascal now addresses the Jesuits directly. Anger and denunciation replace the mocking irony of the first Letters, and instead of exposing new areas of Jesuit impiety, Pascal concentrates mainly on defending his former accusations, refuting all the Jesuit replies to them, point by point, quotation by quotation, detail by detail. These Letters are important to theologians, particularly for Pascal's defence of the Jansenist doctrine of the Eucharist. Yet, superior though they be of their kind, they are far less interesting as literature, and for this reason they are often omitted from editions of the 'Provincial Letters'. The reader is requested, however, not to forget that they were originally there, if only because they suggest the genre to which the work may belong: after 'sufficient' versus 'efficacious' grace and ethics (the consequences of grace in the world), there come refutations of objections—in form the *Provinciales* rejoin that most ubiquitous of theological genres, the treatise.

Perhaps also this sense of form—here it would be simply the feeling that it was time to change tack in order to answer some objections—may have had something to do with Pascal's abandonment of comedy in these Letters. Yet one suspects also that there was more behind this change than this. The fact was that not everyone at Port-Royal had been delighted when Pascal's hilarious Letters began to appear. La mère Angélique Arnauld, the Abbesse of Port-Royal, for example, had been deeply offended by them, and her reason was certainly that there was something not quite suitable in the use of satiric wit in discussions of Christian theology. Moreover, Port-Royal was to campaign for years against the theatre as being wicked and immoral, in fact it was this hostility towards the stage that made Racine turn against them for a time. But then, one might wonder how they could sponsor a work such as the *Provinciales* in which artifice was so important, and which was in essence so theatrical. As Racine angrily pointed out to them, their own 'Provincial Letters' were comedies. Certainly Pascal had found ready answers to the Jesuits who had charged him with making a mockery of holy things, but perhaps also—despite all the quotations from Scripture and the Fathers—Port Royal had felt that at bottom the criticisms were not entirely unjustified; the time had come to treat the issues with all the seriousness befitting them.

The last two Provinciales

Forming a true Conclusion to the *Provinciales* are Letters XVII and XVIII, addressed to Father Annat, S. J., confessor to King Louis XIV. Again one should view them as occasional pieces, for they reflect the intense concern of the Jansenists over recent events.

When Arnauld was formally denounced and censured by the Sorbonne, and it was declared that all students must forswear his errors, a number of Doctors of the Faculty of Theology, in fact some of its most distinguished members, refused to subscribe to these decisions. These theologians were promptly denied the rights and privileges of their office, which meant, among other things, that they might no longer live in their quarters in the University (24 March 1656). The regular meeting of the Assemblée du clergé was still in progress at the time the seventeenth *Provinciale* appeared. The prelates, going far beyond their traditional functions, had made formal declarations condemning the five points. For reasons still not fully understood, the greatest single supporter of the Jansenists, Gondrin, archbishop of Sens, who alone had been causing Mazarin and the Pope more trouble than all the other prelates combined, had suddenly capitulated; he now seemed willing to sign almost anything. Soon the prelates would be drawing up a sort of loyalty oath requiring Churchmen to accept the condemnation of the five points as a condemnation of Jansenius.

In this almost desperate situation, one of the last effective weapons remaining to the Jansenists were the *Provinciales*. No doubt following the advice of Arnauld and Nicole, Pascal now trained his sights on the King's Confessor and attempted, in two masterful Letters, to destroy utterly his reputation. Father Annat was the Jesuit who had claimed in 1654 that the five points were in Jansenius, *totidem verbis*, and had later taken to refuting the *Provinciales*. A bilious writer, with a graceless style, his productions were far below the standard of Father Nouet, S.J., who was also busily answering Pascal's Letters. Yet Annat's unfortunate *'totidem verbis'* made him a temptingly vulnerable target, and for a number of reasons it must be have seemed worth the risk of launching a frontal attack: Father Annat remains a rather shadowy figure in this period at the King's court, quite neglected by historians and theologians alike. Certainly he preferred to work behind the scenes, leaving the more spectacular displays to others such as Mazarin. Yet there is some documentary evidence to suggest that he may have been really a key figure in the condemnation of Jansenism both in the Sorbonne and the Assemblée du clergé.[1] In the manuscript documents of the

[1] See Racine, *Abrégé de l'Histoire de Port-Royal*, ed. A. Gazier (Paris, 1908), pp. 67, 86, 100, 104—110, 121, 185.

D

Mémoires de Beaubrun (B.N., Fonds français, 13896) there is more than one hint that the loud and menacing oratory in the Sorbonne of anti-Jansenists such as the Bishop of Rodez was intended to be heard in Court, above all by Father Annat (fol. 6 recto). There is also evidence that it was not the cynical Mazarin who really cared whether or not the prelates of the Assemblée du clergé condemned the five points, but precisely Father Annat, who helped to engineer the actions of the Assemblée from behind the scenes, even going so far as to persuade the King and Queen to meet with individual delegates and enjoin them to vote against the Jansenists (fol. 503 recto; 506 recto; 508 recto). There was also a more personal reason for Pascal to have chosen Father Annat; sometime earlier, as the fifth *Provinciale* was going to press, Pascal's niece, a nun in the convent of Port-Royal, had been 'miraculously' cured of a fistula on her eye when it was touched by a relic of the Holy Thorn. To Pascal this *miracle de la Sainte-Epine* was a clear sign that God had declared Himself on the side of the Jansenists, and for the miracle to have occurred in his own family strengthened still more his sense of dedication to the cause—a 'superstitious' attitude that the eighteenth-century Encyclopedists would find it difficult to forgive. To Father Annat, on the other hand, this 'miracle', if it proved anything at all—which in his mind was doubtful—showed merely that the time had come for the Jansenists to abandon their false doctrines and return to the orthodox fold.

In Letter XVII, Pascal took his revenge. He casts doubt upon Father Annat's accusation that the Jansenists were 'heretics' by tracing the shifts in meaning ascribed to this word by the Jesuit as the Jansenists disproved one by one his accusations. He then shows that the Confessor of the King of France had not told the truth when claiming the five points were taken from Jansenius in so many words, and associates the spirit of mendacity with the Jesuits generally. He points out that since the question of whether or not the five points are in Jansenius is a mere question of fact, it should be possible to disagree over it, without being charged with heresy, if only because in the past, various Popes and Councils had contradicted one another so frequently over just such questions, a contention that Pascal spells out in concrete examples from Church history both remote and recent. The Jansenists expressly disavow the substance of the five propositions, and if Father Annat expends such effort to make people believe otherwise when the truth is so clear, it suggests that his more sinister purpose may actually be to subvert the doctrine of efficacious grace under the guise of suppressing the alleged 'heresy' of Jansenism. Towards the end, Pascal sorrowfully notes that God had abandoned Father Annat to such a degree that the Jesuit resorted to lies in order to achieve his ends.

Father Annat, who was far from being a mild-mannered theologian, must have become fairly apoplectic when this masterful attack appeared. One senses behind it a concentration and intensity not found to this degree in the preceding Letters. Of course, in a practical sense, Pascal's Letter may have been a mistake, since Father Annat did not wither away under the attack; in fact he wrote a very nasty reply and he remained the King's Confessor, more dedicated than ever to the destruction of Jansenism.

Just before the date of the eighteenth *Provinciale*, the Assemblée du clergé was convoked (17 March 1657) to deliberate on a new Bull of Pope Alexander VII, *Ad sacram Petri sedem*, which again condemned the five points, expressly stating that they were the doctrine of Jansenius, and had been condemned for the meaning the author had intended to give them. The Assemblée voted to receive the Bull, publish it and ordered it enforced in all dioceses. A formulary was attached, to be signed by the prelates within a month:

Je me soumets sincèrement à la constitution du Pape Innocent X du 31 mai 1653 selon son véritable sens, qui a été déterminé par la constitution de notre Saint Père le Pape Alexandre VII du 16 Octobre 1656. Je reconnais que je suis obligé en conscience d'obéir à ces constitutions et je condamne de coeur et de bouche la doctrine des cinq propositions de Cornelius

Jansenius contenue dans son livre intitulé *Augustinus*, que ces deux papes et les évêques ont condamnée; laquelle doctrine n'est point celle de Saint Augustin, que Jansenius a mal expliquée contre le vrai sens de ce docteur. (Quoted in Pierre Blet, *Le Clergé de France et la Monarchie*, II, p. 218)

In some respects the last *Provinciale*, also addressed to Father Annat, is the finest. Of a texture more dense than the rest, it has an extraordinary kind of eloquence, that which comes only in a time of direst urgency, and when there seems to be absolutely nothing to lose. It was related that Pascal had expended immense labour composing it, making as many as thirteen revisions and rewritings. The Jansenists knew it was strong stuff, bound to stir up dissension in the French Church, as well as among the Jesuits, and before sending it to press they tried to use the threat of its publication as a weapon against the formulary recently voted by the Assemblée du clergé. Here again they were over-optimistic in their calculations: for the prelates they approached showed no desire to reach a compromise in order to have Pascal's attack suppressed.

The first part of the Letter again pins Father Annat down concerning the actual sense in which he claims he is condemning the five points attributed to Jansenius. Pascal demands to know why Father Annat persists in calling the Jansenists heretics, since they have expressly disavowed the Calvinist interpretation of these doctrines. (Father Annat was particularly incensed at this part of the Letter, because Pascal pretended that the Jesuit had failed to specify what the Jansenist heresy actually was and wittily expressed surprise at finding out at last that the Jesuit thought the Jansenists were Calvinistic. Father Annat testily, and somewhat flatly, replied that he had already specified the Calvinistic nature of the five points some years before and that surely the Secretary of Port-Royal must have known about it ...)

There follows a masterful exposition of efficacious grace according to the Jansenists, expressed in terms that would be agreeable also to the Thomists,[1] whose doctrines are shown in quotations to be quite similar to their own. But the most striking part of the Letter is Pascal's denial of the authority of the Pope to decide *questions de fait*. In this domain Pascal simply refuses to recognize Papal authority as infallible, and he traces the issue back to its theological source which, to Pascal, was the whole question of the nature of faith. Here the arguments derive from a principle made famous by St Thomas, namely, that Grace does not destroy nature, but perfects it. By the same token, Pascal— probably following Nicole—infers that faith is not established on the ruins of reason, for reason is quite valid in its legitimate sphere of operation. It is rather that faith rises above the limitations of reason.

The implications of this argument are far-reaching: it suggests the possibility of using philosophy—the domain of reason—in matters theological, indeed it suggests that theology must, to some extent, agree with philosophy, or be subject to doubt—a notion which the eighteenth century would be glad to carry to its logical conclusion. In Pascal's work we are still far away from such 'enlightened' inferences, for Pascal limits strictly the application of his principle: for him it is merely a question of factual matters that are clearly known to reason and therefore cannot be denied by Papal bulls. If it is truly certain that the earth is turning, as Galileo maintained it was, all the decrees of the Inquisition will not make it otherwise, and if the five heretical points are not actually in Jansenius, no Papal bull can alter the fact. Nor does the Pope have the right to make men swear they believe something that, through the most elementary operations of reason, they know to be false. For the rest, he argues, it will not be the first time a Pope has been entirely mistaken on a *question de fait*.

More important than the assertion of the necessary continuity between reason and faith—a principle to which even some

---

[1]This ingratiating gesture toward the Thomists—so different from the ironies of the early *Provinciales*—is one of numerous traits suggesting that a significant shift in strategy had taken place since the first letters, and that the influence of the intransigent Arnauld had been superseded by others, such as Nicole, whose approach was more Thomistic.

Jesuits adhered at this time—is Pascal's attitude which implies that one may refuse to obey the Pope and the Holy Office, the Assemblée du clergé and the Sorbonne, and even the express desires of the King of the realm, if such obedience would make one untrue to one's beliefs. Pascal certainly thought he was making his stand within the framework of true Catholicism, and he was merely following in the wake of many a Gallican who had tried to set limits on Papal authority. On the other hand the *Provinciales* (along with Arnauld's defence of the *Version de Mons* and the treatise *De la Foi humaine* attributed to Nicole) were one of the principal pieces of evidence causing the Calvinists to think—quite wrongly, to be sure—that the Jansenists were secretly on their side: Pascal's refusal to accept Papal authority to decide *questions de fait* seemed to reflect their own attitude towards Rome. To them it seemed clear (and here again they ignored the nuances of the text) that Pascal's doctrine of faith was very close to the Calvinist view that faith was a kind of 'persuasion' involving the assent of reason. Pascal does not speak of 'conscience' in this letter; however, he seemed to the Calvinists to be affirming in effect the right of conscience to maintain its convictions despite all the commands of those in authority.

Now, reason and conscience (as opposed to blind obedience to authority) were two of the main elements in the doctrine of religious toleration as it developed in the seventeenth century,[1] and it is not surprising that the first work by a French author devoted expressly to this subject, *Tolérance des Religions* by the Huguenot lawyer Henri Basnage de Beauval (1684), refers to this section of the *Provinciales* when arguing against the use of constraint in matters of faith. Finally we may note that Pascal's statement that if Galileo's theories are correct, all the decrees of the Inquisition will not prevent the earth from turning, seems to be pitting the Church, on the one hand, against physical science, on the other. And even though Pascal is actually more concerned here with the psychology of the act of faith than he

[1]See my monograph, Essays on Pierre Bayle and Religious Controversy (The Hague, 1965), Part II.

is with the defence of Galileo, he gives the impression at least
of anticipating a *prise de position* that would characterize the
whole philosophic movement of the eighteenth century.

No one knows just why Pascal stopped the *Provinciales* with
the Letter XVIII. (There exists a fragment of a Letter XIX, which
was never completed.) Scholars have speculated that Pascal
abandoned the *Provinciales* because of pressure from Port-Royal,
or because the letters, in spite of their success, had proved incapable of achieving their objectives—or because Pascal simply
wanted to devote himself to other Jansenist controversies.
Certainly it could not have been that the Letters had lost their
telling effect: one of the Italian friends of the Jansenists actually
attempted to use the possibility of a nineteenth *Provinciale* as a
threat to make the Papal Nuncio in Paris more favourable to
Jansenist views, and Professor Orcibal suggests that this threat
may have been one of the reasons why the Jansenists gained a
four-year respite from the enforcement of the dreaded formulary.

Whatever the reason for Pascal's turning to other polemics,
the work stands marvellously complete as it is, the two con-
cluding Letters to the King's Confessor picking up all the main
threads: there are reminders of the wickedness of Jesuit casuistry,
brilliant defences of Jansenist grace, flashes of ironic wit, hints
of dialogue, and most unforgettable, a sense of dedication to the
cause, an impassioned expression of determination that would
endure anything fate might bring.

They would need their strength.

Brief Chronology of the Life of Pascal

1623   19 June: birth of Blaise Pascal in Clermont.

1631   Towards the end of the year, the Pascal family moves to Paris.

1640   They move to Rouen, 2 January. Pascal publishes his *Essay pour les Coniques*.

1645   He completes his arithmetical calculating machine (dedicated to Chancellor Séguier).

1646   The Pascal family introduced to Port-Royal through various works of piety written by Jansenists. Pascal experiences his first religious 'conversion' and he repeats Torricelli's experiments on vacuum.

1647   Falling ill, Pascal returns to Paris.
23–24 September: he meets with Descartes.
October: he publishes *Expériences nouvelles touchant le vide*.
November: both he and his sister, Jacqueline, are in contact with Port-Royal.

1648   October: Pascal publishes his *Récit de la grande expérience de l'équilibre des liqueurs*, recounting the experiments of his brother-in-law, Florin Périer, conducted, following Pascal's suggestions, at Puy de Dome.

1650   November: the Pascal family moves back to Paris.

1651   Pascal writes a *Traité du vide*, of which only a few fragments remain.

1652   His sister, Jacqueline, enters Port-Royal, to become a nun there the following year.

1654 Pascal begins composition of a *Traité de l'équilibre des liqueurs*, writes a *Traité du triangle arithmétique* and corresponds with Fermat.

September: frequent visits to Port-Royal to see his sister. 23-24 November: in Paris, the night of Pascal's second religious 'conversion', attested to in the *Mémorial*.

1655 January: a three-week stay in Port-Royal with the 'solitaires'. Pascal's *Entretien avec M. de Sacy* is supposed to have taken place at this time.

1656 January: composition of the first *Provinciale* (dated the 23rd), written probably either at Port-Royal or at Vaumurier, at the estate of the Duc de Luynes. Pascal is 32 years of age.

5 February: the second *Provinciale* (dated 29 January) is being circulated.

6 February: circulation of the third *Provinciale*.

16 February: publication of the censure of Arnauld in the Sorbonne.

25 February: date of the fourth *Provinciale*.

28 March: circulation of the fifth *Provinciale* (dated 20 March). As this *Provinciale* was, presumably, being printed, 24 March, a niece of Pascal was 'miraculously' cured of a fistula on her eye when it was touched by a relic of the Holy Thorn at Port-Royal.

10 April: date of the sixth *Provinciale*.

25 April: date of the seventh *Provinciale*, said to have been read to Louis XIV by his chaplain.

28 May: date of the eighth *Provinciale*.

8 June: Pascal officially attests to the authenticity of the Miracle of the Holy Thorn.

3 July: date of the ninth *Provinciale*.

2 August: date of the tenth *Provinciale*.

18 August: date of the eleventh *Provinciale*.

9 September—4 December: twelfth—sixteenth *Provinciales*.

1657 23 January: date of the seventeenth *Provinciale*.

17 March: the Papal Bull, *Ad sacram . . .*, condemning the five points and declaring them to be the doctrine of Jansenius, is accepted by the Assemblé du clergé.

10-14 May: circulation of the eighteenth *Provinciale* (dated 24 March), after more than a month of fruitless negotiations with Churchmen and delegates to Parlement, offering to suppress this *Provinicale* in exchange for concessions.

1657   6 September: the *Provinciales* placed on the Index in Rome. About this time, Pascal begins composition of notes for an Apology of the Christian Religion, published after his death under the title *Pensées* (1670).

1658   January–July: Pascal collaborates on a series of anti-Jesuit pamphlets, signed 'les Curés de Paris.'

1659   Using a pseudonym, Pascal sends Huygens a *Lettre sur la dimension de lignes courbes*. He becomes seriously ill and is unable to work.

1660   Pascal spends the summer near Clermont; his health improves.

1661   The Assemblée du clergé revives the question of the formulary condemning the five points. A *lettre de cachet* is sent from the King's Council of State to all Bishops demanding that the formulary be signed even by nuns and schoolmasters (23 April). Persecution of Port-Royal begins at this time. The nuns are divided as to whether or not to sign the formulary. Arnauld believes that so long as one distinguishes between 'droit' and 'fait' it is proper to sign. Jacqueline Pascal at first believes it wrong to sign.

22 June: the nuns at Port-Royal, including Jacqueline Pascal, sign; however, the formulary is preceded by a conciliatory *Mandement* from the Vicars General of Paris making the distinction between 'fait' and 'foi'. It is thought by some scholars that Pascal collaborated on this *Mandement*.

1 August: the conciliatory *Mandement* is condemned by

the Pope, as well as by those hostile to the Jansenists in France.

28 November: the nuns sign the formulary again, as they are required to do; however, they add a clause implying they have signed out of humble obedience rather than out of any understanding of the doctrines involved. Pascal does not approve of this signing, because it seems to involve so many 'mental restrictions.' According to certain statements by Arnauld and Nicole it appears that Pascal had come to believe that the Pope and the bishops were actually conspiring to defeat the doctrine of efficacious grace.

1662 January–March: Pascal becomes interested in the establishment of a kind of Parisian bus service, 'les carosses à cinq sols.'

1662 June: Pascal's health is clearly growing worse.

19 August: having received extreme unction two days before, Pascal dies at one o'clock in the morning. He was 39.

A Note on Sources

Since the footnotes in this study are few in number and refer mainly to recent publications, the following additional remarks on bibliography may prove useful.

For the background of the Jesuit controversies, such standard sources as Henri Fouqueray, *Histoire de la Compagnie de Jésus en France*..., 5 vols. (Paris, 1910–1925), especially vols. 4–5; J. M. Prat, *Recherches historiques et critiques sur la Compagnie de Jésus en France du temps du P. Coton*..., 4 vols. (Lyons, 1876), as well as James Brodrick, *The Economic Morals of the Jesuits* London and N.Y., 1934), remain indispensable. There are also a number of helpful articles in the *Dictionnaire de Théologie catholique*. On the Collège de Clermont I consulted notably Gustave Dupont-Ferrier, *Du Collège de Clermont au Lycée Louis-le-Grand* ..., 3 vols. (Paris, 1921–1925) and Pierre Delattre, *Le Collège de Clermont* in *idem*, *Les Etablissements des Jésuites en France*..., vol. III (Enghien, 1955). The discussion of Jesuit doctrines is based mainly on works by Molinists whom Pascal himself singled out for attack. Virtually everything Father Annat wrote is revealing, although not always in the sense intended by the author. (A bibliography of his works may be found in the catalogue of the Bibliothèque nationale, Paris.) Also valuable were works by Jesuits such as Denis Petau, *De la Penitence publique*... (Paris, 1644); François Pinthereau, *De attritionis suffici-*

entia ... (Paris, 1654); Jean de Brisacier, *Le Jansenisme confondu* ... (Paris, 1651); and Antoine Sirmond, *La Defense de la vertu* ... (Paris, 1641). Refutations of the *Provinciales* such as Nicolas Caussin, S. J., *Response anticipée aux dernières Lettres des Jansénistes* ... (Paris, 1656), originally composed as an answer to *La Théologie morale des Jésuites*, and Jacques Nouet, S. J., *Responses aux Lettres Provinciales* ... (Liège, 1658) give insight into the way hostile contemporaries of Pascal interpreted his Letters. For similar reasons one may consult Georges Pirot, S.J., *Apologie pour les casuistes contre les calomnies des Jansénistes* ... (Paris, 1657). The theology of Leonardus Lessius, S.J., especially his *De Gratia* ... (Antwerp, 1610), brings together with exceptional clarity the main traits opposed by the Jansenists.

For those interested in the moral and historical implications of the controversy over casuistry there is an abundant literature. For example, F. Strowski, *Histoire du sentiment religieux en France au XVIIᵉ siècle: Pascal et son temps*, 3 vols. (Paris, 1907); Albert Bayet, *Les Provinciales* ... (Paris, 1929); J. Steinmann, 'Les Provinciales vues par le Père Valensin', *Vie intellectuelle*, *XXVII* (1956), pp. 2–12, and the Introduction to E. Havet's edition of the *Provinciales*, 2 vols. (Paris, 1889).

On the doctrines of Jansenius, there are general discussions in the *Dictionnaire de Théologie catholique*, in *Port-Royal* by Sainte-Beuve, and in what is still the best single source of information concerning the Jansenist–Jesuit controversies: A. de Meyer, *Les Premières controverses jansénistes en France* (1640–1649) (Louvain, 1919). I have also relied on my own study of Jansenius' *Discours de la Réformation de l'Homme intérieur*, and of the *Augustinus*, particularly of those passages later defended by Arnauld and his friends, since their importance to his generation makes these parts authentic 'Jansenism'. Students may wish to consult J. de la Porte, *La Doctrine de Port-Royal*, 2 vols. (Paris, 1922).

On the Jansenist movement in general in both the seventeenth and eighteenth centuries, there is the short study by the late Abbé Cognet, *Le Jansénisme* (Paris: Presses universitaires, 1961) in the 'Que sais-je?' series. On the attrition–contrition controversy one

finds a useful summary in Gabriel Joppin, *Une querelle autour de l'amour pur: Jean-Pierre Camus* ... (Paris, 1938). In addition to his monumental studies on the origins of Jansenism, Professor J. Orcibal's shorter *Saint-Cyran et le Jansénisme* (Paris, 1961) is most helpful. A number of details come from the *Mémoires* of Godefroi Hermant and from the *Histoire du Jansénisme* of René Rapin, S.J. On the papacy, a mine of information is to be found in Father Ceyssens, *La première bulle contre Jansénius* ..., 2 vols. (Brussels, 1961–62). For the Assemblées du clergé I used Pierre Blet, *Le Clergé de France et la Monarchie* ..., 2 vols. (Rome, 1959), together with the original *procès-verbaux* of the meetings that give such a vivid depiction of the events. On the Paris Parlement, there is J. Shennan, *The Parlement of Paris* (London, 1968). For Gallicanism and the Santarelli affair, I used Victor Martin, *Le Gallicanisme politique et le Clergé de France* (Paris, 1929), Aimé-Georges Martimort, *Le Gallicanisme de Bossuet* (Paris, 1953) and the same author's *Le Gallicanisme* (Paris, 1973) in the 'Que sais-je?' series; I have been able to read the unpublished doctoral dissertation of Mr Michael Becker, 'The Santarelli Affair ...' (University of California, Berkeley, 1970) which the author kindly sent me in manuscript.

For the Sorbonne, the first volume of the well-known *Histoire de l'Université de Paris* by Ch. Jourdain, along with Aristide Douarche, *L'Université de Paris et les Jésuites* (Paris, 1888) proved to be the most useful sources. However, for the actual debates on Arnauld, one must consult the manuscripts of the 'Mémoires de Beaubrun' in the Bibliothèque nationale (Fonds français, 13895–13896). An interested student might compose an excellent bibliography of matters relating to the *Provinciales* from the Catalogue of the Pascal exposition held at that library in 1963.

On the *Provinciales* in England: P. Jansen, *De Blaise Pascal à Henry Hammond: Les Provinciales en Angleterre* (Paris: Vrin, 1954), and John Barker, *Strange Contrarieties=Pascal in England* ... (Montreal and London, 1975), Chapter 1. On the *Provinciales* and the traditions of the French *moralistes:* A. J. Krailsheimer, *Studies in Self-interest* ... (Oxford University Press, 1962),

Chapter 6. On Pascal himself, the most valuable single source in French is Professor Jean Mesnard's *Pascal,* 5th ed. (Paris, 1967); in English there is J. H. Broome, *Pascal* (London: Edward Arnold, 1965). On the text of the *Provinciales:* Léon Parcé, *La réimpression des premières Provinciales* in the collective volume *Pascal: Textes du Tricentenaire* (Paris: Fayard, 1963); on their publication: the Introduction by Professor Jean Mesnard in the first volume of his edition of Pascal's *Œuvres complètes* (Paris: Desclée De Brouwer, 1964), pp. 37–41. On style: Patricia Topliss, *The Rhetoric of Pascal* (Leicester University Press, 1966). On the role of the narrator: W.W.E. Slights, 'Patterns and "Personae" . . .', *Kentucky Romance Quarterly,* XIV (1967), pp. 126–138, and, most especially, Harold Weinrich, 'Parler avec vérité, parler avec discrétion . . .', *Sprache im technischen Zeitalter,* XX (1966), pp. 320–326. Two recent studies treat specialized topics: Ronald Schooler, 'L'imagerie érotique dans la 9ᵐᵉ lettre des Provinciales . . .' and William D. Shea, 'L'antithèse clarté-obscurité dans la 12ᵐᵉ Provinciale', both published in *Romance Notes,* XIII (1971), pp. 132–76 and pp. 314–17.

There are two excellent critical editions of the *Provinciales:* the old F. Gazier edition in the 'Grands écrivains de la France' (Paris, 1914), vols. IV–VII, includes valuable historical documentation. The late Abbé Cognet's edition (Paris: Garnier, 1965), conceived on different lines, is informative. A third, and doubtless definitive, critical edition of the *Provinciales* will appear in Professor Jean Mesnard's edition of the *Œuvres complètes* of Pascal. In English there is A. J. Krailsheimer's delightful translation *The Provincial Letters* (Penguin, 1967) and the well-known Introduction to H. F. Stewart's edition (1920).

Acknowledgments

I wish to note that a number of scholars have given me the benefit of their knowledge. Professor J. Orcibal was kind enough to read and comment upon the entire manuscript at an early stage. My loyal friend, Professor Jean Le Corbeiller, did likewise. More recently, I have received useful criticisms from Dr. Will Moore and a number of suggestions from Professor Dale Van Kley. My greatest debt of gratitude is due to Robert Niklaus, Professor Emeritus of the University of Exeter, who suggested this project to me many years ago, and who has faithfully seen it through to the end.